Grandma's Country Cooking

ideals

IDEALS PUBLISHING CORP./11315 WATERTOWN PLANK ROAD/MILWAUKEE, WIS. 53226

Contents

A very special thank you to the following for their cooperation and help in supplying selected recipes from their test kitchens and files:

Alaska Seafood Marketing Institute; American Dairy Association; American Seafood Institute/Wakefield, Rhode Island; Apple Growers of Washington State; Beans of the West; California Fruit Exchange; California Table Grape Commission; California Tree Fruit Agreement; Florida Fruit & Vegetable Association; Growers of Washington State; Gulf & South Atlantic Fisheries Development Foundation, Inc.; Maine Dept. of Marine Resources; National Fisheries Institute/Chicago, Illinois; National Red Cherry Institute/Grand Rapids, Michigan; North Carolina Yam Commission; North West Purple Prune Plum Growers/tested by Pacific Kitchens; Ocean Spray; Oregon, Washington, & California Pear Bureaus/Pacific Bartlett Growers, Inc.; Potato Chip Information Bureau; Sea Grant College Program/Texas Agricultural Extension Service; United Fresh Fruit & Vegetable Association; University of Wisconsin/Sea Grant Institute; Washington State Potato Commission/tested by Pacific Kitchens.

Edited by Julie Hogan

ISBN 0-8249-3033-9

Published by Ideals Publishing Corporation
11315 Watertown Plank Road
Milwaukee, Wisconsin 53226
Published simultaneously in Canada

Cover recipes:
Pork Chops with Corn Bread Stuffing, 20
Fresh Cherry Pie, 59
Sesame Twist, 47

Caramel Corn, 4
Light Peanut Brittle, 61

Appetizers and Snacks

Cheese and Spinach Appetizers

Makes about 5 dozen

    8 ounces feta cheese, crumbled
    1 carton (8 ounces) small curd cottage cheese
    2 eggs, lightly beaten
      Dash garlic salt
    ¼ teaspoon salt
    ⅛ teaspoon white pepper
    ½ pound phyllo *or* strudel dough
    ½ pound butter, melted

In a small bowl, combine cheeses, eggs, salts, and pepper; blend well. Using 1 sheet of dough at a time, brush with melted butter. Repeat with 4 more sheets of dough, placing on top of each other. (Cover unused dough with a damp towel.) Spread filling thinly over half of the layered dough. Roll up, jelly-roll fashion. Place rolls, seam sides down, on a large baking sheet. Brush generously with melted butter. Refrigerate 15 minutes. Use a sharp knife to score chilled dough in diagonal pieces about 1 inch apart, cutting only about ⅛ inch through the dough. Do not cut into filling. Bake 2 rolls at a time at 350° F. 35 to 40 minutes or until golden. Cool before cutting. For best results reheat before serving.

Note: To make triangles, place a single sheet of phyllo dough on a flat surface. Brush with melted butter. Cut lengthwise into 5 equal strips. Place 1 teaspoon filling on the end of each strip about 1½ inches from edge. Fold opposite corner over filling to form a triangle. Repeat folding from left to right (as you would fold a flag) to end of strip. Brush with melted butter. Follow directions for chilling and baking as above.

Crusty Potato Tidbits

Makes about 70

    2 pounds russet potatoes
    2 tablespoons milk
    3 tablespoons butter *or* margarine
    ¼ teaspoon salt
    ⅛ teaspoon black pepper
    1 cup grated Parmesan cheese
    2 tablespoons minced green onion
    2 eggs, lightly beaten
    3 to 4 cups cornflakes, coarsely crushed

Scrub potatoes; cut into quarters. Place potatoes in a large saucepan. Cover with ½ inch salted water. Cover and bring to boiling; reduce heat. Cover and simmer about 20 minutes or until potatoes are tender. Peel potatoes; place in a large bowl. Mash with an electric mixer, gradually beating in milk, butter, salt, and pepper. Add cheese and green onion; blend well. Shape potato mixture into 1-inch balls. Dip balls in eggs, then roll in crushed cornflakes. Place on a greased baking sheet. Bake at 400° F. 10 minutes or until balls are hot and crusty.

Mini Pizzas

Makes 8 servings

    3 tablespoons butter *or* margarine, softened
    4 English muffins, split
    1 can (8 ounces) tomato sauce
    2 tablespoons minced onion
    ¼ teaspoon garlic salt
    ¼ teaspoon crushed leaf oregano
    1 package (10 ounces) precooked sausages, sliced, optional
    ½ cup shredded mozzarella cheese

Spread butter on each muffin half. In a small bowl, combine tomato sauce, onion, garlic salt, and oregano; blend well. Spoon sauce on muffin halves. Arrange sausage slices on top, if desired. Sprinkle cheese over each. Place under broiler 3 minutes or until cheese melts.

Caramel Corn

Makes 5 to 6 quarts

    3 cups packed brown sugar
    1½ cups butter *or* margarine
    ¾ cup white corn syrup
    1½ teaspoons salt
    1½ teaspoons baking soda
    1 teaspoon vanilla
    5 to 6 quarts popped popcorn
    1 can (12 ounces) Spanish peanuts

In a large saucepan, combine brown sugar, butter, and corn syrup; blend well. Bring to boiling over medium heat; boil 5 minutes, without stirring. Remove pan from heat. Add baking soda, salt and vanilla; blend well. Place popcorn in two 13 x 9-inch pans. Drizzle syrup evenly over popcorn. Use two wooden spoons to mix well. Bake at 225° F. 40 minutes, stirring occasionally. Add peanuts; toss lightly to mix. Spread on waxed paper; let stand until cool.

Cranberry Citrus Punch

Makes 36 servings

- 2 bottles (32 ounces each) cranberry juice cocktail, chilled
- 1 can (12 ounces) frozen pink lemonade concentrate, thawed
- 1 can (6 ounces) frozen orange juice concentrate, thawed
- 4 cups cold water
- 1 quart ginger ale, chilled
  Lemon and orange slices

In a large punch bowl, combine cranberry juice cocktail, lemonade and orange juice concentrates, and water; blend well. Just before serving, add ginger ale. Garnish with lemon and orange slices.

Lemonade Refresher

Makes 3 to 4 servings

- 1 cup water
- 1 cup sugar
- 1 cup lemon juice
- 4 cups water

In a saucepan, combine water and sugar. Bring to boiling, stirring constantly until sugar dissolves. Remove from heat. Let stand until cool. Stir in lemon juice and water. Serve over ice cubes.

Hot Buttered Rum

Makes 12 to 14 servings

- 1 cup butter *or* margarine, softened
- ½ cup powdered sugar
- ½ cup packed brown sugar
- 1 teaspoon ground cinnamon
- 1 teaspoon ground nutmeg
- 1 pint vanilla ice cream, softened
- 1 bottle (1 fluid ounce) rum flavoring
  Boiling water
  Cinnamon sticks

In a medium bowl, combine butter, both sugars, and spices; cream with electric mixer until light and fluffy. Beat in ice cream and rum flavoring until smooth. Turn into a 4-cup freezerproof container. Store ice cream mixture in freezer. (Mixture will not freeze solid.) To serve, place ¼ cup ice cream mixture in a mug and add ½ cup boiling water; blend well. Garnish with a cinnamon stick.

Mocha Milk

Makes 6 to 8 servings

- 2 pints coffee ice cream
- ½ cup chocolate-flavored syrup
- ¼ cup instant coffee powder
- 2 quarts milk

In an electric blender or mixer, beat ice cream, syrup, coffee powder, and a small amount of the milk until well blended. Blend in remaining milk. Serve in tall glasses.

Sherbet Slush

Makes 10 to 12 servings

- 1 pint fruit sherbet, slightly softened
- 1 quart ginger ale
- 1 can (15 ounces) pineapple chunks, drained; reserve 1 cup juice

In a large bowl, combine sherbet, ginger ale, and reserved pineapple juice; blend well. Stir in pineapple chunks. Serve in tall glasses.

Pink Grapefruit Punch

Makes 10 servings

- 4 cups grapefruit juice cocktail, chilled
- 4 cups unsweetened pineapple juice, chilled
- 2 cups white grape juice, chilled
  Ice cubes

In a large pitcher, combine all ingredients. Serve over ice cubes.

Hot Mulled Cider

Makes 12 to 16 servings

- 1 cup packed brown sugar
- 2 teaspoons whole allspice
- 2 teaspoons whole cloves
- ⅓ teaspoon salt
  Dash ground nutmeg
- 2 cinnamon sticks
- 1 gallon apple cider
- 1 orange, cut in wedges
  Whole cloves

In a large saucepan, combine brown sugar, allspice, cloves, salt, nutmeg, cinnamon sticks, and cider. Bring slowly to boiling. Cover and simmer 20 minutes. Remove spices with a slotted spoon. Insert a whole clove in each orange wedge. Serve cider in warmed mugs with an orange wedge in each.

Soups

Chicken Gumbo Soup

Makes 8 to 10 servings

   1 stewing hen (4 to 5 pounds)
   1 teaspoon salt
   1 rib celery
   1 carrot, peeled
   1 medium onion
   3 cups diced celery
   3 cups sliced carrots
   2 cups diced onions
      Salt and pepper
   6 chicken bouillon cubes
   ½ cup butter *or* margarine
   ½ cup flour
   1 can (16 ounces) stewed tomatoes
   3 cups cooked rice
   1 can (16 ounces) okra, drained

In a large kettle or Dutch oven, combine chicken, salt, celery rib, carrot, and onion. Add water to cover chicken. Bring to boiling; reduce heat. Cover and simmer 1½ to 2 hours or until chicken is very tender. Skim off scum with a spoon. Discard celery rib, onion, and carrot. Remove chicken from broth; skin and bone. Dice chicken; place in refrigerator. Cool broth to room temperature; place in refrigerator. Remove hardened fat from broth. Return broth to stove. Bring to boiling; reduce heat. Add diced celery, sliced carrots, diced onions, and bouillon cubes. Season with salt and pepper to taste. Cover and simmer about 1 hour or until vegetables are tender. In a large saucepan, melt butter. Stir in flour. Cook over medium heat 3 to 4 minutes, stirring constantly. Gradually add about 2 cups hot broth, stirring with a wire whisk; return to remaining broth. Add tomatoes, rice, okra, and diced chicken. Heat through before serving.

Chili

Makes 6 to 8 servings

   1 tablespoon vegetable oil
   1 pound lean ground beef
   1 large onion, chopped
   1 can (29 ounces) whole tomatoes, undrained
   3 cans (10¾ ounces each) tomato soup, undiluted
   1 tablespoon chili powder
   1 dry red chili pepper, crushed
   1 teaspoon parsley flakes
      Salt and pepper
   1 can (16 ounces) kidney beans, drained

In a skillet, heat oil; brown ground beef and onion; drain fat. In an electric blender or food processor, puree tomatoes and juice. In a large saucepan, combine hamburger mixture, tomatoes, and seasonings. Season with salt and pepper to taste. (If soup is too thick, dilute with a small amount of water.) Cover and simmer about 1½ to 2 hours, stirring occasionally. Add beans during the last 10 minutes cooking time.

Creamy Carrot Soup

Makes 8 to 10 servings

   ¼ cup butter *or* margarine
   ½ cup chopped onion
   ½ cup chopped celery
   4 cups chicken stock *or* broth
   4 cups sliced carrots
   2 cups half-and-half
   ¼ teaspoon ground nutmeg
   ¼ teaspoon black pepper

In a medium saucepan, melt butter. Add onion and celery; sauté until tender. Add stock and carrots; bring to boiling. Cover and simmer 20 minutes or until carrots are tender. Puree carrot mixture in an electric blender or food processor; return to saucepan. Stir in half-and-half, nutmeg, and pepper. Simmer 5 minutes or until heated through.

Mixed Vegetable Soup

Makes 6 servings

   1 package (20 ounces) frozen mixed vegetables
   ¼ cup butter *or* margarine
   1 small onion, minced
   2 tablespoons flour
 2½ cups half-and-half *or* milk *or* combination
   1 cup chicken broth
   1 teaspoon salt
   ⅛ teaspoon black pepper
   ¼ cup chopped parsley

Prepare vegetables according to package directions; drain and set aside. In a large saucepan, melt butter. Sauté onion until tender. Stir in flour; cook 2 minutes or until bubbly, stirring constantly. Gradually stir in half-and-half. Cook until thickened, stirring constantly. Stir in broth. Add vegetables, salt, pepper, and parsley; heat through.

Soups

Swedish Cherry Soup

Makes 6 to 8 servings

- 1 can (16 ounces) pitted red cherries, packed in water
- ½ cup sugar
- 1 orange, sliced
- 1 cinnamon stick
- 6 to 8 whole cloves
- ½ teaspoon lemon juice
- ½ teaspoon cornstarch
- 1 can (20 ounces) sliced peaches, drained; reserve juice

In a large saucepan, combine cherries, sugar, orange, cinnamon stick, cloves, and lemon juice. Bring to boiling; remove from heat. Dissolve cornstarch in a small amount of peach juice. Add remaining juice to cherry mixture; heat through. Slowly stir cornstarch mixture into cherry mixture, stirring constantly. Cook until thickened, stirring frequently. Add peaches. Serve warm or cold as a first course or dessert.

Hamburger Vegetable Soup

Makes 6 servings

- 1 tablespoon vegetable oil
- 1 pound lean ground beef
- ⅔ cup chopped onions
- 1 can (46 ounces) tomato juice
- 2 cans (16 ounces each) mixed vegetables
- 2 beef bouillon cubes
- 1 teaspoon seasoned salt
- 1 teaspoon sugar

Heat oil in a large saucepan; brown ground beef and onions; drain fat. Add remaining ingredients. Bring to boiling; reduce heat. Cover and simmer 30 minutes.

Egg and Lemon Soup

Makes 6 to 8 servings

- 2 quarts chicken broth
- 3 tablespoons butter or margarine
- 1⅓ cups long-grain rice
- 1 teaspoon salt
- ⅛ teaspoon white pepper
- 3 eggs
  - Juice of 1½ large lemons
  - Chopped parsley

In a large saucepan, bring chicken broth and butter to boiling over high heat; reduce heat. Stir in rice, salt, and pepper; return to boiling; reduce heat. Simmer about 15 minutes or until rice is tender. In a small mixing bowl, beat eggs with electric mixer until thick and light-colored. Beat in lemon juice. Gradually stir a little of the hot broth into the eggs. Gradually return egg mixture to broth, stirring constantly. Sprinkle parsley on top of soup and serve.

Bean and Sausage Soup

Makes 4 to 5 servings

- ½ pound (about 1 cup) dry white, navy or Great Northern beans, soaked in water overnight
- 5 cups water
- ½ cup chopped onion
- 1 teaspoon chicken bouillon granules
- ½ teaspoon salt
- ¼ teaspoon ground cumin
- ⅛ teaspoon black pepper
- 1 bay leaf
- ½ pound hot sausage, sliced ½ inch thick
- 1 can (8¾ ounces) garbanzo beans, drained
- 1 can (8¾ ounces) cream-style corn
  - Chopped parsley

Drain and rinse soaked beans. In a large saucepan, combine beans, 5 cups water, onion, bouillon, and seasonings. Cover and simmer about 30 minutes or until beans are almost tender. Add sausage, garbanzo beans, and corn. Return soup to boiling. Cover and simmer 30 minutes or until beans are tender. Discard bay leaf. Garnish with parsley.

Creamy Cheese and Cauliflower Soup

Makes 6 to 8 servings

- 1 medium head cauliflower, broken into flowerets
- ¼ cup butter or margarine
- ¼ cup chopped onion
- ¼ cup flour
- 3 cups hot chicken broth
- 2 cups milk
- 1 teaspoon Worcestershire sauce
- 1 cup shredded sharp process American cheese
  - Minced chives

In a large saucepan, cook cauliflower in a small amount of boiling, salted water 10 to 15 minutes or until tender; drain and chop coarsely. In a large saucepan, melt butter over medium heat. Add onion; sauté until tender. Blend in flour to make a smooth paste. Gradually add broth, stirring constantly. Add milk and Worcestershire sauce. Cook until slightly thickened, stirring frequently. Add cauliflower. Bring to boiling; reduce heat. Stir in cheese. Cook over low heat until cheese melts, stirring constantly. Ladle into serving bowls. Sprinkle each serving with chives.

Eggs and Cheese

Ham and Cheese with Potato Crust

Makes 6 to 8 servings

    Vegetable shortening *or* **butter**
1 **package (24 ounces) frozen hashed brown potatoes, thawed**
⅓ **cup butter** *or* **margarine, melted**
1 **cup shredded Cheddar cheese**
1 **cup shredded Monterey Jack cheese**
1 **cup diced cooked ham**
½ **cup half-and-half** *or* **milk**
2 **eggs**
¼ **teaspoon seasoned salt**

Grease a 9-inch pie plate with vegetable shortening. Press thawed potatoes between paper towels to remove excess moisture. Press potatoes into prepared pie plate, cutting as needed to make a crust. Brush with melted butter. Bake at 425° F. 20 minutes. Remove crust from oven. Layer both cheeses and ham in crust. In a small bowl, combine half-and-half, eggs, and seasoned salt; beat with a fork until well blended; pour over cheese. Bake at 350° F. 35 to 40 minutes or until a knife inserted in the center comes out clean.

Brunch Eggs

Makes 6 servings

3 **slices bacon**
6 **hard-cooked eggs**
1 **can (10¾ ounces) cream of chicken soup, undiluted, divided**
⅛ **teaspoon dry mustard**
    Dash pepper
1 **cup sliced mushrooms**
½ **cup water**
¼ **cup shredded sharp Cheddar cheese**
1 **tablespoon minced chives**
3 **English muffins, split and toasted**

In a large skillet, fry bacon until crisp; drain and crumble; set aside. Reserve 1 tablespoon drippings in skillet. Slice eggs lengthwise in half. Gently remove yolks; place in a small bowl. Use a fork to mash yolks. Add 2 tablespoons soup, mustard, and pepper; blend well. Spoon filling into centers of egg whites. Heat bacon drippings in skillet. Add mushrooms; brown lightly. Stir in remaining soup, water, cheese, and chives. Arrange eggs in soup mixture; reduce heat. Cover and cook until eggs are hot and cheese melts, stirring occasionally. Serve over toasted English muffins.

Bacon and Egg Supreme

Makes 16 servings

½ **cup butter** *or* **margarine**
¼ **cup minced onion**
½ **cup flour**
½ **teaspoon salt**
⅛ **teaspoon black pepper**
4 **cups milk**
1½ **cups shredded Swiss cheese**
16 **hard-cooked eggs, quartered**
1 **cup diced Canadian bacon**
⅓ **cup chopped pimiento**
1½ **cups soft bread crumbs**
3 **tablespoons butter** *or* **margarine, melted**
    Toast points

In a large skillet, melt butter. Add onion; saute' until onion is tender. Stir in flour, salt, and pepper. Gradually add milk, stirring constantly to make a smooth sauce. Add cheese; stir until cheese melts. Place half of the eggs in the bottom of a 3-quart casserole. Sprinkle on half of the bacon and pimiento. Pour half of the sauce over bacon layer. Repeat layers, ending with sauce. Cover and bake at 375° F. 45 minutes. In a small bowl, combine bread crumbs and butter; mix well. Remove cover; sprinkle with buttered bread crumbs. Bake 15 minutes. Serve over toast points.

Milwaukee Rarebit

Makes 4 servings

1 **tablespoon butter** *or* **margarine**
1 **cup chopped onions**
1 **tablespoon Worcestershire sauce**
1 **tablespoon Dijon mustard**
½ **teaspoon paprika**
½ **cup beer**
3½ **cups shredded Cheddar cheese**
2 **teaspoons cornstarch**
12 **cherry tomatoes**
2 **tablespoons chopped parsley**
    Ridged potato chips

In a medium saucepan, melt butter. Sauté onions 3 minutes or until tender. Stir in Worcestershire sauce, mustard, paprika, and beer. In a separate bowl, combine cheese and cornstarch. Gradually stir cheese into beer mixture. Cook until cheese melts and mixture is smooth, stirring constantly. Stir in cherry tomatoes and parsley; heat through. Serve hot in individual bowls with chips for dipping.

No-Fuss Quiche Lorraine

Makes 6 servings

    1½ cups finely crushed potato chips
    1 teaspoon paprika
    1 cup half-and-half
    1 cup whipping cream
    3 eggs, well beaten
    ¼ pound bacon, crisp-cooked, drained, and crumbled
    2 tablespoons sliced green onion
    ¼ teaspoon salt
       Dash black pepper
       Dash nutmeg
    2 cups grated Swiss cheese

In a small bowl, combine potato chips and paprika; blend well. Press chip mixture gently onto bottom and 1½ inches up the sides of an 8-inch springform pan. In a saucepan, heat both creams. Beat into eggs until well blended. Stir in remaining ingredients. Pour egg mixture into crust. Bake at 375° F. 30 to 35 minutes or until a knife inserted in the center comes out clean.

Turkey and Zucchini Rarebit

Makes 6 servings

    ¼ cup butter *or* margarine
    ¼ teaspoon crushed leaf thyme
    6 slices white *or* English muffin bread, toasted
    12 slices turkey *or* chicken
    12 wedges tomato
    12 slices zucchini
    1 envelope (1½ ounces) white sauce mix
    1¼ cups milk
    1 cup shredded Cheddar cheese

In a small saucepan, melt butter. Stir in thyme. Brush toasted bread with herbed butter. Place 2 slices turkey on each bread slice. Alternate 2 tomato wedges and 2 zucchini slices on each. Brush with remaining herb butter. Place on a large baking sheet. Cover with aluminum foil. Bake at 400° F. 10 minutes or until heated through. Prepare white sauce mix in a saucepan according to package directions using 1¼ cups milk. Remove from heat. Add cheese; stir until cheese melts. Spoon sauce over hot sandwiches.

Puffy Omelet

Makes 2 to 3 servings

    4 eggs, separated
    ¼ cup water
    ½ teaspoon salt
       Dash white pepper *or* hot pepper sauce
    1 tablespoon butter
       Sliced fresh fruit, optional

In a small mixing bowl, combine egg whites, water, and salt. Beat with an electric mixer until stiff peaks form. In a separate small bowl, combine egg yolks and pepper. Beat until thick and light-colored. Gently fold yolks into egg whites. Preheat oven to 325° F. In a 10-inch ovenproof skillet, melt butter just until a drop of water sizzles when dropped into the skillet. Pour omelet mixture into skillet. Reduce heat. Gently level surface with a spoon. Cook slowly about 5 minutes or until puffy and lightly browned on the bottom. Lift omelet gently at the edge to judge color. Place in oven and bake 12 to 15 minutes or until a knife inserted in the center comes out clean. Serve with sliced fresh fruit, if desired.

Overnight Cheese Soufflé

Makes 6 to 8 servings

    12 eggs, well beaten
    ½ cup butter, melted
       Salt and pepper
    4 cups milk
    16 slices white bread, crusts trimmed and bread cut in 1-inch cubes
    1½ pounds sharp Cheddar cheese, grated

In a medium bowl, combine eggs, butter, and salt and pepper to taste; blend well. Gradually stir in milk. In an ungreased 2-quart casserole, alternate layers of bread cubes and cheese, ending with cheese. Pour egg mixture over cheese. Cover and refrigerate overnight. Bake at 350° F. 1½ hours or until eggs are set and golden.

Potato Omelet

Makes 2 servings

    1 tablespoon butter *or* margarine
    1 medium potato, peeled and diced
    ⅓ cup minced onion
    2 tablespoons diced green pepper
    ¼ cup catsup
    ½ teaspoon salt
       Dash black pepper
    4 eggs, lightly beaten

In a large skillet, melt butter. Add potato, onion, and green pepper; cook 20 minutes, stirring occasionally. Stir in catsup, salt, and pepper; cook 3 minutes, stirring often. Pour eggs into skillet, tilting pan so that eggs flow around potato mixture. Cook until set. Loosen edges. Fold omelet in half; slide onto serving dish.

Fish and Seafood

Spicy Pan-Fried Fish

Makes 6 to 8 servings

      3 pounds fresh *or* thawed frozen fish fillets *or*
        small pan fish
      1 cup yellow cornmeal
      ½ cup flour
      1½ teaspoons paprika
      1 teaspoon salt
      ½ teaspoon black pepper
      ½ teaspoon celery salt
      ¼ teaspoon dry mustard
      ¼ teaspoon onion powder
      1 cup buttermilk
        Vegetable oil
        Lemon wedges
        Tartar sauce

Cut fillets into serving portions. In a shallow dish, combine cornmeal, flour, paprika, salt, pepper, celery salt, dry mustard, and onion powder; blend well. Dip fish in buttermilk, then dredge in the cornmeal mixture to coat well. In a large skillet, heat oil to 365° F. Fry fish 4 to 5 minutes or until fish flakes easily when tested with a fork, turning to brown both sides. Drain on paper towels. Serve with lemon wedges and tartar sauce.

Broiled Marinated Shrimp

Makes 4 servings

      1½ pounds raw fresh *or* thawed frozen shrimp,
        peeled and deveined
      ⅓ cup lemon juice
      3 tablespoons olive *or* vegetable oil
      3 tablespoons chopped green onions and tops
      2 cloves garlic, minced
      ¾ teaspoon salt
      ½ teaspoon powdered saffron
      ¼ teaspoon black pepper
      ¼ teaspoon crushed leaf thyme
        Chopped parsley
      ½ cup butter *or* margarine

In a 2-quart bowl, combine the first 9 ingredients. Cover and refrigerate 1 hour, stirring occasionally. Drain marinade from shrimp; reserve marinade. Place shrimp in a single layer on a greased broiler pan. Broil 4 inches from heat 5 to 8 minutes or until shrimp are tender. Garnish with chopped parsley. In a 1-quart saucepan, combine reserved marinade and butter. Heat through, stirring to blend. Serve with shrimp.

Crab and Zucchini Quick Dish

Makes 4 servings

      2 tablespoons peanut *or* vegetable oil
      2 cloves garlic, halved
      6 small zucchini, scored and cut in ⅛-inch slices
        (about 1½ pounds)
      ½ pound fresh mushrooms, sliced
      2 pounds king crab legs, cut in 1-inch chunks
      1 can (8 ounces) sliced water chestnuts, drained
      3 tablespoons bottled oyster sauce
      ¼ cup sliced green onion

Heat oil in a large skillet. Add garlic; sauté about 1 minute or until golden. Add half of the zucchini. Cook and stir 2 minutes over medium heat; push to side of pan. Add remaining zucchini; cook and stir 2 minutes; push to side of pan. Add mushrooms; cook and stir 2 minutes; push to side of pan. If pan is too dry, add a little additional oil. Add crab and water chestnuts; cook and stir 1 minute. Add oyster sauce; stir together all ingredients. Transfer to a serving dish. Garnish with green onion.

German-Style Baked Fillets

Makes 4 servings

      1 pound fresh *or* thawed frozen fish fillets
      2 tablespoons margarine *or* vegetable oil
      ½ cup chopped onion
      1 can (27 ounces) sauerkraut, well drained
      ½ cup water
      ½ teaspoon caraway seed
      ½ teaspoon garlic salt
      1 package (3 ounces) cream cheese, cubed
      ½ cup grated sharp Cheddar cheese
      1 tablespoon chopped parsley
        Dark rye bread

Cut fillets into 1-inch pieces. In a large skillet, heat margarine. Add onion; sauté until tender. Add sauerkraut, water, caraway seed, and garlic salt. Cover and simmer 10 minutes or until flavors are well blended. Arrange cream cheese cubes on top of sauerkraut mixture. Top with fish pieces. Cover and simmer 7 minutes or until fish flakes easily when tested with a fork. Sprinkle with grated cheese. Heat until cheese melts. Sprinkle with parsley. Serve with dark rye bread.

Note: Can also be baked in the oven. To do so, layer ingredients in a casserole and bake at 350° F. 20 minutes.

Buttermilk Deep-Fried Fillets

Makes 6 to 8 servings

    2 pounds fish fillets, such as cod, haddock, whiting,
      pollack, *or* hake
    1 cup buttermilk
      Vegetable oil
    1 cup buttermilk baking mix
    2 teaspoons salt
      Lemon wedges, optional
      Malt vinegar, optional

Cut fillets into serving portions. Place fish in a single layer in a shallow baking dish. Pour buttermilk over fish; let stand 30 minutes, turning once. Heat oil for deep frying to 365° F. In a small bowl, combine baking mix and salt. Remove fish from buttermilk, then coat well in baking mix. Deep fry 3 to 4 minutes or until golden brown. Drain on paper towels. Serve with lemon wedges and malt vinegar, if desired.

Note: Can also be fried in a large skillet, turning to brown both sides.

Oysters Williamsburg

Makes 6 to 8 servings

    2 containers (12 ounces each) medium-size
      fresh oysters
      Chicken broth *or* water
    1 tablespoon instant minced onion
    ½ teaspoon paprika
    ½ teaspoon salt
    ¼ teaspoon black pepper
    ⅛ teaspoon garlic powder
    2 teaspoons Worcestershire sauce
    2 tablespoons lemon juice
    ½ cup butter *or* margarine
    ½ cup sifted flour
    ½ cup coarsely chopped ripe olives
    2 or 3 tablespoons cracker crumbs

In a large saucepan, cook oysters in their own juice for 3 to 4 minutes or until edges curl. Remove oysters from pan with a slotted spoon; set aside. Measure oyster liquid. Add chicken broth or water to equal 1½ cups. To oyster liquid, add onion, paprika, salt, pepper, garlic powder, Worcestershire sauce, and lemon juice. In a separate pan, melt butter. Stir in flour, cook over medium heat about 3 minutes, stirring constantly, until mixture turns golden brown. Remove from heat. Slowly stir oyster liquid into flour mixture. Carefully stir in oysters and olives. Turn into a 1½-quart baking dish. Sprinkle cracker crumbs evenly over top. Bake at 400° F. 30 minutes.

Baked Cod with Creamy Vegetable Sauce

Makes 6 servings

    2 pounds fresh *or* thawed frozen cod *or*
      other fish fillets
    2 tablespoons butter *or* margarine, melted
    1 tablespoon lemon juice
    ¾ teaspoon salt
    ½ teaspoon paprika
      Creamy Vegetable Sauce (recipe follows)

Cut fillets into serving portions. Place fish in a greased 13 x 9-inch baking pan. In a small bowl, combine butter and lemon juice; blend well. Drizzle over fish. Sprinkle with salt and paprika. Bake at 350° F. 25 to 30 minutes or until fish flakes easily when tested with a fork, basting with pan juices several times. While fish is baking, prepare Creamy Vegetable Sauce. Spoon sauce over fish.

Creamy Vegetable Sauce

    1 can (10¾ ounces) cream of celery soup, undiluted
    ⅓ cup milk
    ½ teaspoon dry mustard
    1 package (10 ounces) frozen mixed vegetables,
      cooked and drained
    ¼ cup sliced ripe olives
    2 hard-cooked eggs, chopped

In a saucepan, combine soup, milk, and mustard. Cook over low heat, stirring until well blended. Add vegetables, olives, and eggs; blend well; heat through.

Baked Fish and Tomatoes

Makes 4 servings

    1½ pounds fresh *or* thawed frozen fish fillets
    2 teaspoons Dijon mustard
    ¾ teaspoon salt
    ¼ teaspoon black pepper
    2 large tomatoes, peeled and sliced
    1 cup seasoned stuffing mix
    ½ cup grated Parmesan cheese
    ¼ cup butter *or* margarine, melted
      Chopped parsley

Cut fillets into serving portions. Place fish in a single layer in a well greased 1½-quart casserole. Spread mustard over fish. Sprinkle with salt and pepper. Place tomato slices on top of fish. In a small bowl, combine stuffing mix, cheese, and butter; blend well. Spread stuffing mixture over tomatoes. Bake at 325° F. 25 to 30 minutes or until fish flakes easily when tested with a fork. Garnish with chopped parsley.

Stuffed Salmon

Makes 6 servings

  1 fresh *or* thawed frozen salmon *or* trout
    (about 2½ pounds)
    Salt and pepper
  2 cups dry bread cubes
  ⅓ cup minced onion
  ⅓ cup dairy sour cream
  ¼ cup minced dill pickle
  ½ teaspoon paprika
  ½ teaspoon salt
    Dash black pepper
  ¼ cup vegetable oil

Sprinkle fish with salt and pepper to taste. Grease a shallow baking pan; place fish in pan. In a bowl, combine bread cubes, onion, sour cream, pickle, paprika, salt, and pepper. Stuff fish loosely with stuffing mixture. Brush well with oil. Cover with aluminum foil. Bake at 350° F. 45 to 60 minutes or until fish flakes easily when tested with a fork.

Broiled Salmon with Herbed Lemon Butter

Makes 8 servings

  8 fresh *or* thawed frozen salmon fillets
    (about 4 to 6 ounces each)
  ¼ cup butter *or* margarine, melted
  2 tablespoons lemon juice
  2 tablespoons chopped parsley
  ¼ teaspoon dillweed, rosemary, *or* marjoram
  ¼ teaspoon salt
  ⅛ teaspoon black pepper

Line a broiler pan with aluminum foil. Place salmon fillets on greased broiler pan. In a small bowl, combine remaining ingredients. Baste salmon with butter mixture. Broil 4 inches from heat until salmon flakes easily when tested with a fork. (Estimate 10 minutes per inch thickness at thickest portion of salmon.) Do not turn salmon. Baste several times with butter mixture.

Fish Fillets in Barbecue Sauce

Makes 4 to 6 servings

  1½ pounds fresh *or* thawed frozen fish fillets
    Salt and pepper
  2 tablespoons vegetable oil
  ½ cup chopped onion
  ½ cup catsup
  ¼ cup packed light brown sugar
  3 tablespoons Worcestershire sauce
  1½ teaspoons chili powder
  1 teaspoon salt
  ⅛ teaspoon black pepper

Cut fillets into serving portions. Season to taste with salt and pepper. In a large skillet, heat oil. Brown fish on both sides. In a bowl, combine onion, catsup, brown sugar, Worcestershire sauce, chili powder, salt, and pepper; blend well. Pour over fish. Cover and simmer 15 minutes or until fish flakes easily when tested with a fork.

Oven-Fried Perch Fillets

Makes 3 to 4 servings

  2 tablespoons butter *or* margarine
  ½ cup wheat germ
  ½ cup toasted bread crumbs
  1 pound perch fillets
  ½ cup milk
  2 tablespoons butter *or* margarine, melted
    Salt and pepper
    Tartar sauce, optional

Butter an 11 x 7-inch baking pan with 2 tablespoons butter; set aside. On a piece of waxed paper, lightly mix wheat germ and bread crumbs. Dip fillets in milk, then in crumb mixture to coat well. Place fillets in prepared pan, skin side down. Drizzle melted butter over fish. Season with salt and pepper to taste. Bake at 500° F. 10 minutes or until fish flakes easily when tested with a fork. Serve with tartar sauce, if desired.

Poached Fish Fillets with Cheese Sauce

Makes 2 to 4 servings

  1 cup milk, divided
  2 tablespoons dry sherry
  ¼ teaspoon Worcestershire sauce
  ½ teaspoon salt
    Dash black pepper
  1 pound fish fillets
  1 tablespoon flour
  ¾ cup grated sharp Cheddar cheese

Cut fillets into serving portions. In a large skillet, combine ¾ cup of the milk, sherry, Worcestershire sauce, salt, and pepper; blend well. Heat until simmering. Add fish fillets; cover and poach until fish flakes easily when tested with a fork. Use a slotted spatula to carefully remove fish to a serving platter. Cover with aluminum foil. In a small bowl, combine remaining ¼ cup milk and flour; blend well. Use a wire whisk to gradually blend into poaching liquid over low heat. Add grated cheese; stir until cheese melts and sauce is thickened. Pour over fillets and serve.

Fish Fillets in Barbecue Sauce

Meat

Swiss Steak with Cheese

Makes 4 servings

  1 beef round steak (about 2 pounds)
  3 tablespoons flour
  ¼ cup butter *or* margarine
  2 cans (16 ounces each) tomatoes, undrained
2½ teaspoons salt
  ½ teaspoon crushed leaf basil
  ¼ teaspoon black pepper
  1 cup chopped onions
  1 cup chopped green pepper
1½ cups shredded mozzarella cheese

Cut steak into serving portions. Dredge in flour to coat well. In a large skillet, melt butter. Brown meat slowly on both sides. Add tomatoes and liquid, salt, basil, and pepper; break up tomatoes with a spoon. Cover and simmer 1 hour. Add onions and green pepper; simmer 30 minutes or until steak is tender. Sprinkle cheese evenly over steak. Cook until cheese melts.

Stuffed Round Steak

Makes 8 to 10 servings

  1 beef round steak (about 2½ pounds), fat trimmed
  ½ cup soy sauce
  ½ cup water
  ½ cup dry sherry
  1 tablespoon brown sugar
  2 tablespoons lemon juice
  2 tablespoons vegetable oil
  ¼ teaspoon hot pepper sauce
  1 clove garlic, crushed
  ¼ teaspoon black pepper
    Bread *or* Rice Stuffing (recipes follow)
  1 tablespoon cornstarch

Place steak between 2 sheets of plastic wrap or waxed paper. Flatten with a mallet or rolling pin to about ⅛-inch thickness. Peel off plastic wrap. In a shallow glass baking pan, combine soy sauce, water, sherry, brown sugar, lemon juice, oil, hot pepper sauce, garlic, and pepper; blend well. Place steak in marinade. Cover and refrigerate at least 2 hours, turning occasionally. Prepare Bread or Rice Stuffing. Drain marinade from steak; reserve marinade. Pat steak dry with paper towels. Spoon stuffing onto steak, spreading to within ½ inch of all edges. Roll up lengthwise; secure with wooden picks and string. Return to baking dish with marinade. Cover and bake at

350° F. 1½ hours or until steak is tender, basting occasionally with marinade. Place stuffed steak roll on a cutting board. Remove wooden picks and string. In a small saucepan, dissolve cornstarch in a small amount of marinade. Stir in remaining marinade. Cook over low heat until slightly thickened, stirring constantly. Slice steak roll; arrange slices on a serving platter. Spoon sauce over steak slices and serve.

Bread Stuffing

  3 tablespoons butter *or* margarine
  ¼ cup chopped onion
  ½ cup sliced celery
  ⅔ cup sliced water chestnuts
  ⅔ cup sliced bamboo shoots
  ½ cup chopped mushrooms
  6 cups toasted white bread cubes
  ⅔ cup chicken broth
  ½ cup half-and-half
  2 tablespoons chopped parsley
  1 teaspoon salt
  ¼ teaspoon black pepper
  ½ teaspoon crushed leaf sage
  ¼ teaspoon crushed leaf marjoram
  ¼ teaspoon ground thyme

In a large saucepan, melt butter. Add onion, celery, water chestnuts, bamboo shoots, and mushrooms; sauté until onion and celery are tender. Add remaining ingredients; blend well.

Rice Stuffing

  ¼ cup butter *or* margarine
  ½ cup chopped water chestnuts
  ½ cup sliced mushrooms
  ½ cup chopped celery
  ¼ cup chopped green onions
2½ cups cooked rice
  1 cup bean sprouts, rinsed and drained
  ½ cup chicken broth
  2 tablespoons chopped parsley
  2 tablespoons chopped pimiento
  1 teaspoon salt
  ⅛ teaspoon black pepper
  ½ teaspoon ground ginger

In a large saucepan, melt butter. Add water chestnuts, mushrooms, celery, and green onions; sauté until celery is tender. Add remaining ingredients; blend well.

Skillet Meat Loaf

Makes 6 servings

- 1½ pounds lean ground beef
- ¼ pound ground pork
- ¼ pound ground veal
- 2 eggs, lightly beaten
- 1 cup soft bread crumbs
- ¼ cup chopped onion
- 1 tablespoon Worcestershire sauce
- 2 teaspoons salt
- 1 teaspoon celery salt
- ¼ teaspoon black pepper
- 2 tablespoons catsup
- ½ cup fine dry bread crumbs
- 2 tablespoons butter *or* margarine
- 2 tablespoons vegetable oil

In a large bowl, combine ground beef, pork, and veal; blend well. Add eggs, soft bread crumbs, onion, Worcestershire sauce, both salts, pepper, and catsup; blend well. Shape meat mixture into an oval loaf. Coat loaf with dry bread crumbs. In a large skillet, heat butter and oil. Add meat loaf. Cover and cook over medium-low heat 30 minutes. Turn meat loaf over. Cook 30 minutes or until meat is no longer pink and meat loaf is well browned.

Deviled Steak Strips

Makes 5 to 6 servings

- 1 beef round steak (about 1½ pounds), fat trimmed, cut in 2-inch strips
- ¼ cup flour
- 3 tablespoons vegetable oil
- ¼ cup chopped onion
- 1 clove garlic, minced
- 1½ cups water, divided
- ½ cup tomato sauce
- 1 tablespoon vinegar
- 1 teaspoon prepared horseradish
- 1 teaspoon prepared mustard
- ¾ teaspoon salt
- ¼ teaspoon black pepper
  Hot noodles *or* fluffy rice

In a shallow dish, dredge steak strips in flour to coat well. In a large skillet, heat oil. Brown meat, onion, and garlic. Stir in 1 cup of the water, tomato sauce, vinegar, horseradish, mustard, salt, and pepper. Cover and simmer 1 hour or until meat is tender, stirring occasionally. Add remaining ½ cup water. Stir to scrape browned bits from bottom of pan with a spoon. Serve over noodles or rice.

Sliced Beef and Gravy

Makes 10 to 12 servings

- 1 beef rump roast (4 to 5 pounds)
- 4 cups water
- 4 beef bouillon cubes
- ½ cup flour
- 2 large onions, sliced
  Salt and pepper

Place roast on a rack in a roasting pan. Roast, uncovered, at 325° F. 1½ hours. Cool to room temperature. Cover and refrigerate overnight. Remove roast from pan; reserve drippings. Cut roast into thin slices; set aside. In a medium saucepan, bring water to boiling. Add beef bouillon cubes; stir until dissolved. In a large skillet, heat reserved drippings. Add flour; blend well. Cook and stir over low heat until brown and thickened. Gradually add bouillon, stirring constantly until thickened. Return a layer of sliced beef to roasting pan. Season with salt and pepper to taste. Place a layer of sliced onion on top of meat; season with salt and pepper. Repeat layers until all beef and onions are used. Pour gravy over all. Bake at 350° F. 1½ hours or until beef is tender.

Saucy Meat Loaf

Makes 8 servings

- 2 pounds lean ground beef
- ½ cup chopped green pepper
- ½ cup chopped celery
- ½ cup chopped onion
- 2 eggs, lightly beaten
- 1 package (1½ ounces) dry tomato soup mix
- ½ cup dry bread crumbs
- ½ cup milk
  Salt and pepper
- 1 can (15 ounces) tomato sauce
- 2 cans (4 ounces each) mushroom stems and pieces, drained
- ⅔ cup water
- 2 tablespoons brown sugar

In a large bowl, combine ground beef, green pepper, celery, onion, eggs, soup mix, bread crumbs, milk, and salt and pepper to taste; blend well. Shape into a loaf. In a small bowl, combine tomato sauce, mushrooms, water, and brown sugar; blend well. Pour sauce over top of meat loaf. Bake at 350° F. 50 to 60 minutes or until meat loaf is no longer pink inside.

Meat

Roast Venison with Sour Cream Gravy

Makes 6 to 8 servings

2½ cups dry red wine
½ cup apple cider
3 bay leaves
4 whole peppercorns
1 venison roast (about 6 pounds)
    Salt
¼ cup butter *or* margarine
    Sour Cream Gravy (recipe follows)

In a shallow dish, combine wine, apple cider, bay leaves, and peppercorns. Place venison in marinade. Cover and refrigerate overnight, turning occasionally. Drain marinade from roast; reserve 1 cup marinade. Place roast on a rack in roasting pan, fat-side up. Sprinkle with salt to taste. Insert a meat thermometer in the thickest part of the roast, without touching bone or fat. Roast at 325° F. 25 minutes per pound and to desired doneness. While venison is baking, combine butter and reserved marinade in a saucepan. Cook over low heat until butter melts, stirring occasionally. Brush heated marinade over roast during the last 30 minutes of roasting time. Remove roast to warmed serving platter. Prepare Sour Cream Gravy. Serve gravy with roast.

Sour Cream Gravy

1½ tablespoons flour
½ teaspoon salt
¾ cup pan drippings from roast
½ cup dry red wine
1 cup dairy sour cream

In a medium saucepan, combine flour and salt. Gradually add drippings. Stir in wine. Cook over medium heat until thickened, stirring constantly. Reduce heat to low. Stir in sour cream and heat through but do not boil.

Steak and Kidney Pie

Makes 6 servings

1 beef kidney
¼ cup flour
1 teaspoon salt
⅛ teaspoon black pepper
1 pound beef round steak, cut ¾ to 1 inch thick, cubed
3 tablespoons vegetable oil
1 medium onion, chopped
¼ cup chopped, drained pimiento
2 tablespoons Worcestershire sauce
¼ teaspoon ground thyme
1½ cups water
    Piecrust for 9-inch pie (recipe on page 57)

Wash kidney, remove tubes and fat. Cut kidney into 1-inch cubes. In a pie plate, combine flour, salt, and pepper. Coat steak and kidney cubes in flour mixture; reserve remaining flour. In a large skillet, heat oil. Brown meat cubes; remove from pan and set aside. Add onion to skillet; sauté until tender. Drain drippings from skillet. Add pimiento, Worcestershire sauce, thyme, and water to onion; bring to boiling. Add browned meat and any remaining flour mixture; mix lightly; set aside. Roll out dough on a lightly floured surface to a 10-inch circle. Invert pie plate over dough; cut a circle about 1 inch larger than pie plate. Cut a design in crust to vent steam. Cut a second circle inside the first about 1 inch from the edge to make a circular pastry strip to line the edge of the pie plate. Moisten edge of pie plate with water. Fit outer pastry circle into inside edge of pie plate. Transfer meat mixture to pie plate. Cover with top crust. Seal top pastry to inside edge; flute edge. Bake at 325° F. 1½ hours or until golden. If crust is browning too rapidly, cover edge with aluminum foil.

Beef and Onions

Makes 6 servings

⅓ cup olive *or* vegetable oil
1 lean beef chuck *or* rump roast (2 pounds), fat trimmed and cut in 1-inch cubes
3 pounds small onions
1 tablespoon mixed pickling spices
1 small bay leaf
1 can (6 ounces) tomato paste
1¼ cups hot water
2 cloves garlic, minced
1 tablespoon salt
¼ teaspoon black pepper
½ cup vinegar

In a large saucepan or Dutch oven, heat oil. Add meat; brown slowly, about 20 minutes, stirring to brown all sides. Peel onions; set aside. Combine pickling spices and bay leaf in a cheesecloth bag; tie securely. In a small bowl, combine tomato paste and water; blend well. Add to meat along with spice bag, garlic, salt, and pepper. Place onions on top of beef. Pour vinegar over all. Liquid should half cover ingredients. If not, add more water. Place a heavy plate upside down on top of onions. Bring to boiling; reduce heat. Cover and simmer 2 hours or until meat and onions are tender and liquid is reduced to gravy consistency. Discard spice bag before serving.

Meat

Roast Pork with Pears

Makes 4 servings

    Orange Marinade (recipe follows)
1 boneless pork loin roast (3 pounds)
3 Bartlett pears, peeled and halved
    Orange slices, optional
    Hot cooked rice

Prepare Orange Marinade; reserve ¼ cup. Place pork roast in a roasting pan without a rack; brush with remaining marinade. Refrigerate at least 1 hour. Roast at 325° F. 1½ to 1¾ hours or until 180° to 185° F. on a meat thermometer, basting occasionally with pan juices. Brush pear halves with reserved marinade. Place in roasting pan during the last 15 minutes of roasting time. Serve roast with hot pears garnished with orange slices, if desired. Serve with hot rice.

Orange Marinade

Makes 1 cup

  ½ teaspoon salt
  2 teaspoons cornstarch
  ⅔ cup orange juice
  ¼ cup lemon juice
  2 tablespoons vegetable oil
  2 cloves garlic, minced
  1 tablespoon crushed leaf oregano

In a small saucepan, combine salt, cornstarch, and orange juice; stir to dissolve cornstarch. Stir in lemon juice. Cook over medium-high heat about 1 minute or until mixture thickens. Remove from heat. Stir in oil, garlic, and oregano. Let stand until cool.

Lamb Shank Ragout

Makes 4 servings

  3 strips bacon, cut in 1-inch pieces
  4 lamb shanks *or* 2 pounds boneless lamb, fat trimmed
  2 teaspoons salt
  1 teaspoon celery salt
  ½ teaspoon black pepper
  2 carrots, sliced
  1 rib celery, sliced
  1 medium onion, chopped
  3 tablespoons flour
  1 can (6 ounces) tomato paste
  2 cups water
  1 cup red wine *or* beef stock
  1 bay leaf, crumbled
  ¼ teaspoon dried mint leaves
  ¼ teaspoon ground cinnamon

In a Dutch oven, cook bacon until fat is transparent. Remove bacon from pan. Add lamb; brown on all sides. Remove lamb from pan. Add salts, pepper, carrots, celery, and onion; sauté until onion is tender; drain fat, reserving 2 tablespoons. Stir flour into vegetable mixture; blend well. Return bacon and lamb to pan. Stir in tomato paste, water, and wine; bring to boiling. Stir in bay leaf, mint, and cinnamon. Simmer 1 hour 45 minutes.

Sunday Baked Ham

Makes 6 servings

  ½ fully-cooked smoked ham (about 5 pounds)
    Whole cloves
  1 can (8 ounces) jellied cranberry sauce
  2 tablespoons thawed frozen orange juice concentrate
  ¼ cup packed brown sugar
  1 tablespoon vinegar
    Pinch ground cloves

Place ham on a rack in a roasting pan. Bake at 325° F. 30 minutes. Remove from oven. Trim excess fat and rind with a sharp knife. Score fat in a diamond pattern. Insert cloves where points meet. In a small saucepan, combine cranberry sauce, orange juice concentrate, brown sugar, vinegar, and ground cloves. Bring to boiling; reduce heat. Simmer 2 minutes, stirring constantly. Brush glaze on ham; return to oven. Bake 1 hour, brushing with glaze every 15 minutes. Let stand 10 minutes before slicing.

Pork Chops with Corn Bread Stuffing

Makes 6 servings

  ¼ cup butter *or* margarine
  1 small onion, chopped
  ½ cup chopped celery
  1½ cups water
  1 package (6 ounces) corn bread stuffing mix
  6 thick rib pork chops, pockets cut in each
  2 tablespoons vegetable oil
  ¾ cup chicken broth
    Sautéed Apples (page 41)

In a saucepan, melt butter. Sauté onion and celery until just tender. Stir in water and seasonings from stuffing mix. Cover and simmer 5 minutes. Remove from heat. Stir in stuffing mix. Stuff pork chops; secure with wooden picks. In a large skillet, heat oil. Brown chops on both sides. Place in a 12 x 8-inch baking pan. Cover and bake at 350° F. 30 minutes. Add broth. Bake, uncovered, 30 minutes or until tender. Place Sautéed Apples on a platter. Arrange chops on top.

Country Chicken

Makes 6 servings

- ¼ cup butter *or* margarine
- 4 whole chicken breasts, halved and boned
- 2 cloves garlic, crushed
  Seasoned salt
  Dash black pepper
- 1 can (16 ounces) whole tomatoes, chopped; reserve liquid
- ½ cup sauterne *or* chicken broth
- 2 tablespoons chopped parsley
- 1 tablespoon cornstarch dissolved in ¼ cup water

In a large skillet, melt butter. Add chicken breasts and garlic; brown on both sides. Transfer chicken breasts to a 2-quart casserole. Season with salt and pepper to taste. In the same skillet chicken was browned in, combine tomatoes, sauterne, parsley, and cornstarch mixture; bring to boiling. Pour over chicken. Cover and bake at 350° F. for 35 to 40 minutes or until chicken breasts are tender.

Honeyed Chicken

Makes 4 servings

- 1 broiler-fryer chicken (2½ to 3 pounds), cut up
- 1 cup honey
- ½ cup butter *or* margarine
- ¼ cup lemon juice
- 1 teaspoon salt

In a 13 x 9-inch baking pan, place chicken, skin side up. In a small saucepan, combine honey, butter, lemon juice, and salt; blend well. Heat over low heat until bubbly. Baste chicken with honey mixture. Bake at 325° F. 2 to 2½ hours or until chicken is tender, basting every half hour.

Almond Chicken

Makes 4 servings

- 2 tablespoons vegetable oil
- 2 whole chicken breasts, halved
- 1 can (15 ounces) tomato sauce
- 1 jar (8 ounces) peach preserves
- 2 tablespoons chopped onion
- 1½ tablespoons soy sauce
- ¼ teaspoon ground ginger
- ½ cup toasted sliced almonds

In a large skillet, heat oil. Add chicken; brown well; drain fat. In a small bowl, combine tomato sauce, preserves, onion, soy sauce, and ginger; blend well. Pour sauce over chicken. Cover and simmer 1 hour or until chicken is tender, turning once. Place chicken on a serving platter. Spoon sauce over chicken. Garnish with toasted almonds.

Oven-Fried Chicken

Makes 6 to 8 servings

- ½ cup flour
- 1 teaspoon salt
- ½ teaspoon paprika
- ¼ teaspoon black pepper
- 6 to 8 chicken parts (2 breasts, halved and 4 legs and thighs)
- ½ cup butter *or* margarine, melted

In a paper bag, combine flour, salt, paprika, and pepper. Add chicken pieces, 1 at a time; shake to coat evenly. Dip both sides of chicken in melted butter. Place chicken in a single layer, skin side down, in a 13 x 9-inch baking pan. Bake 30 minutes; turn chicken skin side up. Bake at 400° F. for 20 to 30 minutes or until chicken is tender.

Golden Chicken Bake

Makes 8 servings

- ½ cup butter *or* margarine, divided
- 1 pound mushrooms, sliced
- 4 cups chopped cooked chicken
- 1 cup sliced ripe olives
- 6 tablespoons flour
- ½ teaspoon salt
- ⅛ teaspoon black pepper
- 2 cups hot chicken stock *or* broth
- 12 slices white bread, cut in 3-inch rounds
  Butter
- 1½ cups grated sharp Cheddar cheese

In a saucepan, melt ¼ cup of the butter. Add mushrooms; cook 10 minutes or until tender; drain liquid. In a 12 x 8-inch baking dish, layer chicken, mushrooms, and olives. In a small saucepan, melt remaining ¼ cup butter. Add flour, salt, and pepper; stir until bubbly and golden. Gradually add chicken stock; cook until thickened, stirring constantly. Pour sauce over chicken mixture. Brush bread rounds lightly with butter. Toast in oven until lightly browned. Arrange toast over chicken. Sprinkle cheese on top. Bake at 350° F. 30 minutes or until heated through and cheese melts.

Poultry

Crisp Corn-Breaded Chicken

Makes 8 servings

- ½ cup yellow cornmeal
- ½ cup flour
- 1½ teaspoons salt
- 1 teaspoon dillweed
- ¼ teaspoon garlic salt
- ¼ teaspoon black pepper
- 2 broiler-fryer chickens (2 to 3 pounds each), cut up
  Milk
- ½ cup butter *or* margarine, melted

In a shallow dish, combine cornmeal, flour, salt, dillweed, garlic salt, and pepper. Dip chicken in milk, then in cornmeal mixture to coat well. Place chicken in two 13 x 9-inch baking pans; let stand 10 minutes. Drizzle butter over chicken. Bake at 375° F. 55 to 60 minutes or until chicken is tender and golden brown.

Chicken Breasts and Grapes

Makes 4 servings

- ½ teaspoon salt
- ½ teaspoon paprika
- ⅛ teaspoon black pepper
- 2 large chicken breasts, skinned, boned, and split
- 1 tablespoon butter *or* margarine
- ⅛ teaspoon crushed leaf rosemary
- 1 cup chicken broth
- 2 tablespoons chopped onion
- 1 tablespoon cornstarch dissolved in 1 tablespoon cold water
- ½ cup green *or* red grapes, halved; seeded, if necessary

In a small dish, combine salt, paprika, and pepper. Rub chicken breasts with spices. In a large skillet, melt butter; brown chicken slowly, turning once. Turn chicken, skin side up; sprinkle with rosemary. Add chicken broth and onion to chicken. Cover and simmer 20 minutes or until chicken is tender. Stir cornstarch mixture into skillet; cook until slightly thickened, stirring constantly. Add grapes; cook and stir until sauce boils. Remove from heat. Place chicken on a serving platter. Pour sauce over chicken.

Peachy Spiced Chicken

Makes 4 servings

- 1 broiler-fryer chicken (2½ to 3 pounds), quartered or cut up
- 2 peaches, quartered
- 1 can (8 ounces) sliced water chestnuts, drained
- ¼ cup soy sauce
- ¼ cup water
- ½ cup chopped onion
- 1½ teaspoons minced gingerroot
- 1 clove garlic, crushed
- ½ teaspoon cinnamon
- ¼ teaspoon ground allspice
- ¼ teaspoon anise seed, crushed
- ⅛ teaspoon ground cloves

Place chicken in a shallow baking dish. In a medium bowl, combine peaches, water chestnuts, soy sauce, water, onion, gingerroot, and garlic; blend well. Pour over chicken. Cover and refrigerate 2 or 3 hours, turning twice. Remove peaches; set aside. Reserve marinade. Arrange chicken in a 13 x 9-inch baking dish. Pour marinade over chicken. In a small dish, combine cinnamon, allspice, anise seed, and cloves; blend well. Sprinkle spices over chicken. Bake at 350° F. 40 minutes, basting twice with reserved marinade. Add peaches; bake 20 minutes or until chicken is tender and peaches are heated through. Place chicken on a serving platter. Spoon peaches and sauce on top and serve.

Hearty Chicken and Potatoes

Makes 4 servings

- 1 broiler-fryer chicken, (2½ to 3 pounds), cut in serving pieces
- 4 potatoes, peeled and cut in pieces
- 1 onion, minced
- 1 clove garlic, minced
- 1 teaspoon salt
- ¼ teaspoon black pepper
  Paprika
- 2 tablespoons vegetable oil

In a large bowl, combine chicken, potatoes, and onion. Sprinkle with garlic, salt, pepper, and paprika. Drizzle oil over all; toss lightly to coat with oil. Arrange chicken and potatoes in a baking dish. Bake at 350° F. 1 hour or until chicken and potatoes are tender.

Poltry

Robust Country Chicken

Makes 4 servings

- ¼ cup flour
- 1½ teaspoons salt
- ¼ teaspoon black pepper
- 1 broiler-fryer chicken (2½ to 3 pounds), cut in serving pieces
- ¼ cup vegetable oil
- ½ cup chicken broth
- 2 tablespoons snipped parsley
- 1 can (16 ounces) butter beans
- 1 can (12 ounces) whole kernel corn, drained
- 1 tablespoon chopped drained pimiento
- 2 cans (8 ounces each) tomato sauce with mushrooms
- 1 teaspoon seasoned salt

In a pie plate, combine flour, salt, and pepper. Dredge chicken in flour mixture to coat well. In a large skillet, heat oil. Lightly brown chicken on all sides; drain fat. Add broth. Cover and simmer 40 minutes. Add parsley, butter beans, corn, pimiento, tomato sauce, and seasoned salt. Simmer 10 minutes or until chicken is tender.

Turkey with Sausage Stuffing

Makes 12 servings

- 1 frozen turkey (8 to 15 pounds), thawed
- 1 bag (16 ounces) seasoned stuffing mix
- 1 loaf white or whole wheat bread, torn into pieces and dried overnight
- ½ cup butter or margarine
- 8 ounces bulk pork sausage
- 8 ounces mushrooms, sliced
- 1 cup chopped celery
- 1 cup chopped onions
  Boiling water
- 3 eggs, lightly beaten
  Melted butter

Remove neck and giblets from turkey; reserve for other uses. Rinse turkey; pat dry with paper towels. In a large skillet, brown sausage. Push sausage to side of pan. Add mushrooms, celery, and onion; sauté until vegetables are tender-crisp. Drain fat; set aside. In a large bowl, combine stuffing mix and dry bread. Cut butter into pieces; add to stuffing mixture. Pour enough boiling water over bread to moisten as desired. Add sausage and vegetable mixture; blend well. Add eggs; blend well. Lightly stuff neck and body cavity. Secure neck skin to back of turkey. Tie legs and wings to body. Truss opening. Place turkey in roasting pan. Brush with melted butter. Cover turkey with aluminum foil tent, and roast 3½ to

5½ hours at 325° F. or until 185° F. on a meat thermometer inserted between leg and thigh. Baste with melted butter during roasting time. Remove foil ½ hour before end of roasting time to brown bird well. Let stand 20 minutes before carving. Remove all stuffing from cavity before refrigerating leftover turkey.

Old Fashioned Chicken and Dumplings

Makes 8 servings

- 2 broiler-fryer chickens (2½ to 3 pounds, each), cut in serving pieces
- 4 cups water
- 4 ribs celery, cut in pieces
- 1 cup sliced carrots
- 1 cup chopped onions
- 2 tablespoons snipped parsley
- ⅛ teaspoon ground thyme
- ⅛ teaspoon black pepper
  Fluffy Dumplings (recipe follows)
- 1 cup water
- ½ cup flour
- 1 teaspoon salt
- ¼ teaspoon black pepper

In a Dutch oven, combine chickens, water, celery, carrots, onions, parsley, thyme, and pepper. Bring to boiling; reduce heat. Simmer, covered, 1 to 1½ hours or until chicken is tender; skim fat with a spoon or refrigerate until fat hardens on surface. Prepare Fluffy Dumplings. Return chicken stock to boiling. Cover pan and return to boiling; reduce heat. Simmer 12 to 15 minutes or until dumplings are dry and fluffy. *Do not lift cover.* Arrange dumplings and chicken on a serving platter. Measure 4 cups chicken stock into a medium saucepan. In a small bowl, combine water, flour, salt, and pepper; blend until smooth. Bring stock to boiling. Gradually stir in flour mixture. Cook until gravy thickens, stirring constantly. Pour gravy over chicken and dumplings.

Fluffy Dumplings

- 1½ cups flour
- 1 tablespoon minced parsley
- 2 teaspoons baking powder
- ½ teaspoon salt
- ⅔ cup milk
- 2 tablespoons vegetable oil
- 1 egg, lightly beaten

In a medium bowl, combine flour, parsley, baking powder, and salt. Stir in milk, oil, and egg just until moistened.

Roast Duck with Bing Cherries

Makes 2 to 3 servings

- 1 can (17 ounces) pitted dark cherries, drained
- 1 cup port wine
- 1 frozen duckling (about 4 pounds), thawed
- 1 teaspoon salt
- 2 oranges, quartered
- 3 whole peppercorns
- 1 clove garlic, minced
- ¼ cup minced onion
- ½ cup flour
- 1½ cups chicken broth
- ¼ cup currant jelly

In a bowl, combine cherries and wine; set aside. Sprinkle duck inside and outside with salt. Prick well with a fork. Place oranges and peppercorns in cavity. Truss opening. Place duck, breast up, on a rack in a roasting pan. Bake, uncovered, at 425° F. 30 minutes. Reduce heat to 375° F. Bake 1½ hours or until duck is tender; drain fat; reserve ¼ cup drippings. Place duck on a serving platter. Cover with aluminum foil; set aside. In a saucepan, heat reserved drippings. Sauté garlic and onion until tender. Remove from heat. Stir in flour and broth until smooth. Return to heat. Bring to boiling; reduce heat. Cook until thickened, stirring constantly. Stir in cherries and wine and jelly. Cook until jelly melts, stirring constantly. Serve sauce with duck.

Apple Stuffed Cornish Hens

Makes 6 servings

- 6 frozen Cornish game hens, thawed
- 3 tablespoons butter or margarine
- 1 cup chopped celery
- ½ cup chopped onion
- 6 cups dry bread cubes
- 1 teaspoon poultry seasoning
- ½ teaspoon salt
- ¼ teaspoon black pepper
- ⅛ teaspoon allspice
- 2 cups chopped, unpeeled apples
- ¼ cup raisins

Rinse hens; pat dry with paper towels. In a large skillet, melt butter. Sauté celery and onion until tender. Stir in bread cubes, seasonings, apples, and raisins; toss lightly to mix. Lightly stuff hens with apple mixture. Press wings to breast; tie with string. Tie legs together. Place on a rack in a roasting pan. Bake at 350° F. 1½ hours or until tender, basting occasionally with drippings. Remove strings before serving.

Roast Goose with Raspberry Sauce

Makes 6 servings

- 1 goose (8 to 10 pounds)
- ½ lemon
  Salt and pepper
- 1 apple, cored and cubed
- 1 orange, quartered
- 1 onion, sliced
- 1 tablespoon butter or margarine
- ½ cup red or black raspberry jelly
  Juice of ½ lemon
- ½ cup water
- ¼ cup port wine
- 1 cinnamon stick

Rinse goose; pat dry with paper towels. Sprinkle inside and outside with salt and pepper. Rub with cut side of lemon. Place apple, orange, and onion in cavity. Truss opening. Place goose on a rack in a roasting pan. Bake at 325° F. 20 to 25 minutes per pound and until juices run clear when tested with a fork. Place goose on a serving platter; discard stuffing. Cover with aluminum foil. Let stand 15 minutes. To make sauce, combine jelly, lemon juice, water, wine, and cinnamon stick in a saucepan. Simmer 5 minutes, stirring occasionally. Serve with goose.

Chicken and Cheese Rolls

Makes 4 servings

- 2 whole chicken breasts, skinned, boned, and cut in halves
  Salt and pepper
- 2 slices Monterey Jack cheese, cut in halves
- 2 tablespoons flour
- 2 eggs, lightly beaten
- ¼ cup dry bread crumbs
- ¼ cup chicken broth
- 2 tablespoons butter or margarine
- 2 teaspoons snipped parsley
- ¼ teaspoon crushed leaf marjoram

Flatten chicken breasts between pieces of plastic wrap until about ⅛ inch thick. Sprinkle with salt and pepper to taste. Place 1 piece of cheese on each breast half. Fold in sides; roll up. Secure with wooden picks. Roll chicken in flour, then dip in egg. Roll in bread crumbs to coat. Place rolls in an 11 x 7-inch baking dish. Bake, uncovered, at 350° F. 30 minutes. Prepare sauce. In a small saucepan, combine broth, butter, parsley, and marjoram. Cook over low heat until butter melts, stirring often. Pour sauce over rolls. Bake 10 minutes or until chicken is tender. Remove wooden picks before serving.

Casseroles and Skillet Meals

Patchwork Casserole

Makes 12 servings

- 2 pounds lean ground beef
- 2 green peppers, chopped
- 1 large onion, chopped
- 1 package (2 pounds) frozen southern-style hashed brown potatoes
- 2 cans (8 ounces each) tomato sauce
- 1 can (6 ounces) tomato paste
- 1 cup water
- 1 teaspoon salt
- ½ teaspoon crushed leaf basil
- ¼ teaspoon black pepper
- 1 pound process American cheese, thinly sliced

In a large skillet, brown ground beef until no longer pink, breaking up with a spoon; drain fat. Add green peppers and onion; sauté until tender. Add potatoes, tomato sauce, tomato paste, water, salt, basil, and pepper; blend well. Spoon half of meat and potato mixture into a 13 x 9-inch baking dish or two 1½-quart casseroles. Cover with half of the cheese. Top with remaining meat and potato mixture. Cover with aluminum foil. Bake at 350° F. 45 minutes. Remove foil. Cut remaining cheese into decorative shapes. Arrange cheese in a patchwork design on top. Let stand 5 minutes or until cheese melts.

Best Lasagna

Makes 8 servings

- 1 pound lean ground beef *or* ½ pound *each* ground beef and ground pork
- 2 cloves garlic, minced
- 3 tablespoons parsley flakes, divided
- 1 teaspoon crushed leaf basil
- 1 teaspoon crushed leaf oregano
- 3 teaspoons salt, divided
- 1 can (16 ounces) tomatoes, undrained
- 1 can (15 ounces) tomato sauce
- 10 lasagna noodles
- 3 cups ricotta *or* small curd cottage cheese
- 2 eggs, lightly beaten
- ½ teaspoon black pepper
- ½ cup grated Parmesan cheese
- 1 pound mozzarella cheese, thinly sliced

In a large skillet, brown ground beef until no longer pink, breaking up with a spoon. Add garlic, 1 tablespoon parsley flakes, basil, oregano, 1 teaspoon salt, tomatoes and juice, and tomato sauce; blend well. Simmer 30 minutes, stirring occasionally. Prepare lasagna noodles according to package directions; rinse, drain and set aside. In a bowl, combine ricotta cheese, eggs, remaining 2 tablespoons parsley flakes, 2 teaspoons salt, pepper, and Parmesan cheese; blend well. Spoon a little of the meat sauce mixture over the bottom of a 13 x 9-inch baking dish. Arrange half of the cooked lasagna noodles in a single layer in baking dish. Spread half of the cheese mixture, half of the mozzarella cheese, and half of the meat sauce over noodles. Repeat layers, ending with mozzarella cheese. Bake at 350° F. 45 minutes or until bubbly and cheese is golden. Let stand 15 minutes before serving.

Beef and Rice

Makes 8 servings

- 3 tablespoons butter *or* margarine
- 1 large onion, minced
- 1½ pounds lean ground beef
- 1½ teaspoons salt
- ¼ teaspoon black pepper
- 1 can (16 ounces) peas, drained
- 1 can (4 ounces) mushroom stems and pieces, drained
- 2 cans (10¾ ounces each) tomato soup, undiluted
- 2 cups cooked rice
- 4 slices bacon

In a large saucepan, melt butter. Add onion, ground beef, salt, and pepper; cook about 10 minutes, stirring often; drain fat. Add peas, mushrooms, soup, and rice; blend well. Turn into a 1½-quart casserole. Lay bacon slices over top. Bake, uncovered, at 350° F. about 1 hour or until hot and bubbly.

Red Links Casserole

Makes 6 servings

- 1½ pounds pork sausage links
- 6 small whole onions
- 1 can (10¾ ounces) tomato soup, undiluted
- ¼ cup chili sauce
- 6 medium potatoes, peeled and cut in 1-inch cubes
- Salt and pepper

In a large skillet, brown sausage links well on all sides. Remove from skillet; drain fat. Cut sausage into 1-inch pieces. Add onions to skillet; brown lightly. Stir in tomato soup and chili sauce, blending well. Add potatoes. Season with salt and pepper to taste. Cover and bring to boiling; reduce heat. Simmer about 40 minutes or until potatoes are tender.

Casseroles and Skillet Meals

Beef and Mushroom Casserole

Makes 4 servings

2 tablespoons butter *or* margarine
1 medium onion, chopped
4 cups coarsely chopped cooked beef
2 cloves garlic, minced
1½ cups sliced mushrooms
2 cups coarsely chopped tomatoes
½ cup sliced ripe olives, optional
½ teaspoon salt
½ teaspoon crushed leaf thyme
¼ teaspoon black pepper
4 cups cooked noodles
1 cup shredded Cheddar cheese

In a large skillet, melt butter. Add onion; sauté until tender. Add beef; cook over medium heat until heated through. Add remaining ingredients; mix lightly. Transfer to a greased 2-quart casserole. Bake at 350° F. 20 to 30 minutes or until heated through.

Chow Mein Casserole

Makes 4 servings

2 tablespoons butter *or* margarine
2 green onions, sliced
1 green pepper, cubed
1 rib celery, chopped
1 clove garlic, minced
2 cups chicken broth
¼ cup cornstarch
2 tablespoons soy sauce
1 tablespoon molasses
½ teaspoon salt
Dash white pepper
2 tablespoons dry white wine *or* chicken broth
2 cups diced roast pork
1 can (16 ounces) Chinese mixed vegetables, rinsed and drained
1 can (3 ounces) chow mein noodles

In a small saucepan, melt butter. Sauté green onions, green pepper, celery, and garlic until vegetables are tender-crisp. In a medium saucepan, combine broth, cornstarch, soy sauce, molasses, salt, and pepper; stir to dissolve cornstarch. Cook over low heat until thick and clear, stirring constantly. Stir in wine. Add cooked vegetable mixture, pork, and mixed vegetables; stir lightly. Transfer to a buttered 1½-quart casserole. Sprinkle chow mein noodles around edge of casserole. Bake at 350° F. 20 minutes or until heated through.

Sausage and Sweet Potato Casserole

Makes 4 servings

1 can (18 ounces) sweet potatoes, sliced 1 inch thick
1 can (20 ounces) pineapple chunks, drained; reserve ¼ cup syrup
1 package (12 ounces) smoked link sausage, cut in 1-inch pieces
3 tablespoons brown sugar
2 tablespoons cornstarch
¼ teaspoon salt
1 tablespoon butter *or* margarine

In a buttered 11 x 7-inch baking dish, arrange potatoes, pineapple, and sausages. In a small saucepan, combine brown sugar, cornstarch, and salt. Add enough water to reserved pineapple syrup to equal 1 cup liquid. Gradually blend liquid into cornstarch; stir to dissolve cornstarch. Cook over medium heat until thick and bubbly, stirring constantly. Add butter; stir until butter melts. Pour sauce over potatoes, pineapple, and sausage. Cover with aluminum foil. Bake at 350° F. 1 hour or until bubbly.

Veal and Pork Hot Dish

Makes 8 to 10 servings

1 veal steak (about 1 pound), cut in cubes
1 pork steak (about 1 pound), cut in cubes
4 cups water
2 teaspoons salt
1 small onion, sliced
6 ounces wide egg noodles (about 3¼ cups)
1 can (16 ounces) peas, drained
½ pound process American cheese, diced
1 can (10¾ ounces) cream of chicken soup, undiluted
1 can (10¾ ounces) cream of mushroom soup, undiluted
1 jar (2 ounces) pimiento, drained and diced
1 green pepper, diced
1 cup crushed potato chips, divided

In a large saucepan, combine veal and pork steak cubes, water, salt, and onion. Bring to boiling; reduce heat. Simmer about 45 minutes or until meat is tender. Add noodles; mix lightly. Cook 15 to 20 minutes or until noodles are tender. Add peas, cheese, both soups, pimiento, and green pepper; heat through. Add more water if mixture is too thick. Divide meat and noodle mixture between two buttered 1½-quart casseroles. Sprinkle half of potato chips on top of each. Bake, uncovered, at 350° F. 45 minutes or until heated through.

Corned Beef Deluxe

Makes 6 servings

    ½ cup butter *or* margarine, divided
    ¼ cup flour
    1 teaspoon salt
    ⅛ teaspoon black pepper
    2 cups milk
    2 cups shredded process American cheese
    1 cup thinly sliced onions
    2 cups thickly sliced cooked potatoes
      Salt and pepper
      Paprika
    1 can (12 ounces) corned beef, sliced
    4 hard-cooked eggs, halved
    ⅓ cup soft bread crumbs

In a large saucepan, melt 4 tablespoons butter. Add flour, salt, and pepper. Cook until bubbly, stirring constantly. Gradually add milk, stirring constantly. Cook over medium heat until thickened, stirring constantly. Remove from heat. Add cheese; stir until cheese melts. In a skillet, melt 2 tablespoons butter. Add onions; sauté until onions are tender. In a 2-quart casserole, place potato slices. Season to taste with salt, pepper, and paprika. Pour about one-third of the cheese sauce over the potatoes. Arrange corned beef slices on top of potatoes. Top with onions and half of the remaining sauce. Arrange egg halves, cut sides up, over corned beef. Pour remaining sauce over eggs. In a small bowl, combine bread crumbs and remaining 2 tablespoons butter; blend well. Sprinkle over top of casserole. Bake at 350° F. 45 minutes or until heated through.

Beef and Noodle Jackpot

Makes 8 servings

    2 tablespoons vegetable oil
    1 pound lean ground beef
    ¼ cup minced onion
    1 can (10¾ ounces) tomato soup, undiluted
    1½ cups water
    4 ounces medium egg noodles (about 2¼ cups)
    1½ teaspoons salt
    ⅛ teaspoon black pepper
    1 can (16 ounces) cream-style corn
    ¼ cup chopped ripe olives
    1 cup grated process American cheese, divided

In a large skillet, heat oil. Add ground beef and onion; sauté until ground beef is no longer pink; drain fat. Add soup, water, and noodles; blend well. Cover and bring to boiling; reduce heat. Simmer about 20 minutes, stirring occasionally.

Add salt, pepper, corn, olives, and ½ cup of the cheese; blend well. Pour into a greased 2-quart casserole. Sprinkle with remaining ½ cup cheese. Bake, uncovered, at 350° F. about 45 minutes or until heated through.

Beef Casserole with Sour Cream Puffs

Makes 6 to 8 servings

    ¼ cup vegetable oil
    1 beef round steak (about 1 pound), cut in
      ½-inch strips
    1½ cups chopped onions
    2 tablespoons flour
    1 cup chopped tomatoes
    1 cup water
    1 can (6 ounces) tomato paste
    1 tablespoon sugar
    1½ teaspoons salt
    ¼ teaspoon black pepper
    ½ teaspoon Worcestershire sauce
    1½ cups sliced mushrooms
    ¾ cup dairy sour cream
      Sour Cream Puffs (recipe follows)
      Half-and-half *or* milk
      Sesame seed

In a large skillet, heat oil. Brown meat well on all sides. Add onions; sauté 3 minutes. Add flour; cook until onions are tender, stirring often. Add tomatoes, water, tomato paste, sugar, salt, pepper, and Worcestershire sauce. Cover and simmer 1½ hours or until meat is tender, stirring occasionally. Add mushrooms and sour cream. Cook over low heat 5 minutes or until heated through; do not boil. Place meat mixture in a 2-quart casserole. Arrange Sour Cream Puffs on top. Brush half-and-half on puffs. Sprinkle with sesame seed. Bake, uncovered, at 425° F. 20 to 25 minutes.

Sour Cream Puffs

    1¼ cups flour
    2 teaspoons baking powder
    ½ teaspoon salt
    ¼ cup vegetable shortening
    ¾ cup dairy sour cream

Sift flour, baking powder, and salt into a mixing bowl. Cut in shortening with a pastry blender or two knives until consistency of fine crumbs. Add sour cream; blend with a fork until a stiff dough forms. Gather into a ball. Roll out dough on a floured surface to ½-inch thickness. Cut out 6 to 8 rounds with a 2½-inch biscuit cutter. Cut out 6 to 8 rounds with a 1-inch biscuit cutter. Top each larger round with a smaller round.

Veal and Sour Cream Casserole

Makes 8 to 10 servings

     6 tablespoons butter *or* margarine, divided
 1½ pounds boneless veal, cut in chunks
   ¾ cup minced onions
     1 can (8 ounces) sliced mushrooms, undrained
     8 ounces wide egg noodles (about 4½ cups)
     1 cup dairy sour cream
     1 teaspoon salt
   ¼ teaspoon black pepper
   ¼ cup crushed cornflakes

In a large skillet, heat 4 tablespoons butter. Add veal and onions; sauté until veal is browned and onions are tender. Add mushrooms and liquid. Simmer about 30 minutes, stirring occasionally. In a large saucepan, bring 2 quarts salted water to boiling. Add noodles; cook 8 to 10 minutes or until tender. Drain and rinse in cold water. In a buttered 2-quart casserole, combine noodles, meat mixture, sour cream, salt, and pepper; stir lightly to blend. Top with crushed cornflakes. Dot with remaining 2 tablespoons butter. Bake, uncovered, at 350° F. 30 to 40 minutes or until heated through.

Wurst with Dilled Potatoes

Makes 4 servings

     4 large potatoes
     4 slices bacon, cut in pieces
     1 medium onion, chopped
   ½ cup chopped celery
   ½ cup chopped dill pickles
     1 pound knackwurst
     1 cup dill pickle liquid
     4 teaspoons sugar
   ½ teaspoon caraway seed
   ½ teaspoon dry mustard
   ½ teaspoon salt
     2 tablespoons chopped parsley

Cook unpeeled potatoes in boiling salted water 15 to 20 minutes or until almost tender. Peel and cut into thick slices. In a large skillet, partially cook bacon. Add onion, celery, and pickles. Cook until onion and celery are tender, stirring often. Stir in potatoes, knackwurst, pickle liquid, sugar, caraway seed, dry mustard, and salt. Cover and simmer until potatoes are tender and knackwurst is heated through, turning occasionally with a spatula. Serve from skillet or transfer to a serving platter. Slice knackwurst before serving. Sprinkle with parsley.

Scallops and Fish

Makes 4 to 5 servings

   ½ pound fresh *or* thawed frozen scallops
   ½ pound fresh *or* thawed frozen haddock fillets
     3 tablespoons butter *or* margarine
     1 small onion, diced
     2 ribs celery, diced
   ½ green pepper, diced
     1 can (10¾ ounces) cream of shrimp soup, undiluted
     1 can (5.5 ounces) evaporated milk
     1 jar (2 ounces) pimientos, drained
   ½ cup soft bread crumbs
     2 tablespoons butter, melted

Cut fillets into serving portions; set aside. Cut scallops into halves; set aside. In a large skillet, melt 3 tablespoons butter. Sauté onion, celery, and green pepper until tender. Place fish on top of onion mixture. Cover and simmer 5 minutes. Add scallops. Cover and simmer 5 minutes. Stir in soup, milk, pimientos, and salt and pepper to taste. Transfer to a greased 1½-quart casserole. Cool to room temperature. Refrigerate overnight to blend flavors. In a small bowl, combine bread crumbs and melted butter; blend well. Sprinkle crumbs over top of casserole. Bake at 350° F. 30 to 40 minutes or until heated through.

Shrimp Casserole

Makes 4 servings

     3 tablespoons butter *or* margarine
   ¾ pound raw fresh *or* thawed frozen shrimp,
        peeled and deveined (cut large shrimp in half)
   ⅓ cup chopped celery
   ¼ cup chopped green pepper
   ¼ cup chopped onion
     1 can (10¾ ounces) cream of celery *or* cream of
        mushroom soup, undiluted
   ⅓ cup sliced water chestnuts, drained
     1 hard-cooked egg, chopped
     1 tablespoon lemon juice
   ¼ teaspoon salt
   ½ cup seasoned stuffing mix
   ¼ cup shredded Cheddar cheese

In a large skillet, melt butter. Add shrimp, celery, green pepper, and onion. Cook over medium heat until shrimp and vegetables are tender, stirring often. Add soup, water chestnuts, egg, lemon juice, salt, and stuffing mix; blend well. Transfer to a buttered 1½-quart casserole. Bake at 350° F. 20 minutes. Sprinkle cheese on top. Bake 10 minutes or until cheese melts.

Casseroles and Skillet Meals

Stuffed Shells

Makes 6 to 8 servings

1½ pounds lean ground beef
½ pound bulk Italian sausage
1 large onion, chopped
1 clove garlic, minced
3 cups shredded mozzarella cheese
½ cup Italian seasoned dry bread crumbs
¼ cup chopped parsley
1 egg, lightly beaten
Salt and pepper
18 jumbo pasta shells, cooked until almost tender and drained
2 jars (15½ ounces each) spaghetti sauce
½ cup dry red wine
½ cup grated Parmesan cheese

In a large skillet, brown ground beef and Italian sausage. Add onion and garlic; sauté until onion is tender; drain fat. Stir in mozzarella cheese, bread crumbs, parsley, egg, and salt and pepper to taste; blend well. Fill pasta shells with meat mixture. Spoon about ¼ of the spaghetti sauce over the bottom of a 13 x 9-inch baking dish. Arrange shells on top of sauce. Blend wine into remaining spaghetti sauce; pour over shells. Sprinkle Parmesan cheese on top. Bake at 400° F. 20 to 25 minutes or until bubbly.

Turkey Strata

Makes 8 servings

2 tablespoons butter or margarine
½ cup chopped onion
1½ cups leftover chicken or turkey gravy or 1 can (10½ ounces)
6 eggs, lightly beaten
½ cup milk
½ cup grated Parmesan cheese, divided
½ teaspoon paprika
¼ teaspoon crushed leaf rosemary
10 slices bread
2 cups cubed cooked turkey or chicken
1 package (10 ounces) frozen chopped broccoli, cooked and drained

In a medium saucepan, melt butter; sauté onion until tender. Stir in gravy, eggs, milk, ¼ cup Parmesan cheese, paprika, and rosemary; blend well. Cut bread slices into four triangles; reserve 4 triangles. In a buttered 12 x 8-inch baking dish, arrange remaining bread. Sprinkle turkey and broccoli over bread. Top with reserved triangles. Pour egg mixture over bread. Sprinkle with remaining cheese. Cover and refrigerate overnight. Bake at 350° F. 45 minutes or until eggs are set.

Chicken Tetrazzini

Makes 6 to 8 servings

2 tablespoons butter or margarine
1 onion, minced
2 cups sliced mushrooms
2 tablespoons lemon juice
Salt and pepper
⅛ teaspoon grated nutmeg
1 can (10¾ ounces) cream of mushroom soup, undiluted
1 can (10¾ ounces) golden mushroom soup, undiluted
2 soup cans half-and-half or milk
1 cup grated American cheese
¼ cup dry sherry or chicken broth
1 pound pasta rings
4 cups cubed cooked chicken or turkey

In a large saucepan, melt butter. Sauté onion until tender. Add mushrooms and lemon juice; cook 4 minutes, stirring often. Season with salt and pepper to taste and nutmeg. Stir in both soups and half-and-half; heat through, stirring often. Add cheese; cook until cheese melts, stirring constantly. Remove from heat. Stir in wine; set aside. Cook pasta rings according to package directions; drain. Place half of the pasta rings in a buttered, shallow, 3-quart baking dish. Spread chicken evenly over pasta. Add remaining pasta rings, spreading evenly. Pour sauce on top to cover pasta and chicken. Bake, uncovered, at 375° F. 30 minutes or until golden and bubbly.

Turkey and Potato Bake

Makes 4 servings

¼ cup butter or margarine
¼ cup flour
½ teaspoon salt
⅛ teaspoon black pepper
1¼ cups milk
2 cups shredded sharp Cheddar cheese, divided
2 cups chopped cooked turkey or chicken
1 package (10 ounces) frozen peas, cooked and drained
2 cups hot mashed potatoes

In a medium saucepan, melt butter. Stir in flour, salt, and pepper; cook 2 minutes, stirring constantly. Gradually add milk. Cook until thickened, stirring constantly. Add 1½ cups of the cheese; stir until cheese melts. Stir in turkey and peas. Transfer to a buttered 2-quart casserole. Spoon potatoes around edge of casserole. Bake at 350° F. 35 minutes. Top with remaining ½ cup cheese. Bake until cheese melts.

Vegetables

Stuffed Yams

Makes 6 servings

- 6 medium yams
- Vegetable oil
- 2 tablespoons butter *or* margarine
- ½ cup half-and-half *or* milk
- 2 tablespoons brown sugar
- 2 tablespoons grated Parmesan cheese
- ¾ teaspoon salt
- ¼ teaspoon ground nutmeg
- 1 egg, lightly beaten

Wash and dry yams; lightly oil skins. Bake at 350° F. 1 hour or until tender. Cut yams lengthwise in half; scoop out pulp; reserve shells. Place pulp in mixing bowl; mash with an electric mixer. Beat in butter, half-and-half, brown sugar, cheese, salt, and nutmeg. Spoon mashed yams into reserved shells. Brush tops with egg. Bake at 400° F. 15 minutes or until lightly browned.

Winter Vegetable Stew

Makes 10 to 12 servings

- 1 tablespoon vegetable oil
- ¼ cup chopped onion
- 1 clove garlic, crushed or minced
- ½ cup sliced carrot
- 1½ cups halved new potatoes
- 1 teaspoon crushed leaf basil
- ¼ teaspoon salt
- ⅛ teaspoon black pepper
- 1½ cups apple juice
- 2 cups coarsely chopped cabbage
- 1 cup green beans, cut in 1½-inch pieces
- 1 cup sliced zucchini
- 1 cup chopped tomatoes
- 1 cup green pepper strips
- 1 tablespoon flour
- ½ cup water

In a large saucepan, heat oil. Add onion and garlic; sauté 1 minute. Add carrot, potatoes, basil, salt, pepper, and apple juice. Bring to boiling; reduce heat. Cover and simmer 15 minutes. Add cabbage, green beans, zucchini, tomatoes, and green pepper. Bring to boiling; reduce heat. Cover and simmer about 10 minutes or until vegetables are just tender. In a small bowl, combine flour and water; blend until smooth. Stir flour mixture into stew; cook about 1 minute or until thickened, stirring constantly.

Basil Celery

Makes 6 servings

- 1 stalk (bunch) celery
- ¼ cup butter *or* margarine
- 1 cup diced carrots
- 1 cup diced green pepper
- ¾ cup chopped onions
- 1¼ cups diced tomatoes
- 1 teaspoon cornstarch
- ½ cup chicken broth
- 2 tablespoons chopped parsley
- 2 teaspoons crushed leaf basil

Trim tops from celery to 6 inches from base; remove leaves from tops. (Use leaves in soups, stews, etc.) Cut enough of the tops to make 1 cup diced celery; set aside. Cut celery ribs into 6 lengthwise wedges; set aside. In a small skillet, melt butter. Add carrots, green pepper, onions, and reserved diced celery; sauté for 5 minutes. Spoon into a 12 x 8-inch baking pan. Stir in tomatoes. Arrange reserved celery wedges over vegetables. In a small bowl, dissolve cornstarch in chicken broth. Stir parsley and basil into broth; pour over celery wedges. Cover and bake at 350° F. about 35 minutes or until celery is tender.

Fresh Corn Pudding

Makes 6 servings

- 1 tablespoon cornstarch
- ½ teaspoon sugar
- ¾ teaspoon salt
- Dash black pepper
- 1 cup milk, divided
- 3 eggs, lightly beaten
- 4 to 5 ears corn, husked and kernels scraped from cobs *or* 2½ cups frozen
- 1 tablespoon butter *or* margarine
- ⅓ cup minced onion
- ¼ cup minced green pepper

In a medium bowl, combine cornstarch, sugar, salt, and pepper. Stir in 2 tablespoons of the milk; blend until smooth. Stir in remaining milk. Blend in eggs and corn. In a small skillet, melt butter. Add onion and green pepper; sauté until vegetables are tender. Stir into corn mixture. Pour into a buttered 1½-quart casserole. Place casserole in a larger pan. Pour enough hot water into outer pan to reach the height of the corn mixture. Bake at 350° F. about 1 hour or until a knife inserted in the center comes out clean.

Vegetables

Green Beans with Sour Cream Sauce

Makes 4 servings

 1½ cups dairy sour cream *or* plain yogurt
 ⅓ cup chopped parsley
 3 tablespoons lemon juice
 3 tablespoons Dijon mustard
   Salt and pepper
 1 pound fresh green beans, cut in 2-inch pieces
   Butterhead lettuce
   Capers
   Chopped parsley

In a small bowl, combine sour cream, parsley, lemon juice, mustard, and salt and pepper to taste; blend well. Refrigerate until well chilled. Cook beans in boiling salted water until just tender; drain and chill. To serve, arrange lettuce on a serving platter. Arrange beans on top of lettuce. Spoon sauce into center of platter. Garnish with capers and parsley.

Jeweled Acorn Squash

Makes 4 servings

 2 medium acorn squash
 2 tablespoons butter *or* margarine
 2 tablespoons flour
 ¾ cup orange juice
 3 tablespoons lemon juice
 ¼ cup packed brown sugar
 ¾ teaspoon salt
 ⅛ teaspoon black pepper
 ½ cup halved, seeded dark grapes
 ¼ cup halved seedless green grapes

Cut squash lengthwise in half; scoop out seeds. Place squash, cut sides down, in a shallow baking dish. Pour in ½ inch hot water. Bake at 375° F. 45 minutes or until squash is tender. In a small saucepan, melt butter. Blend in flour until smooth. Stirring constantly, add orange juice, lemon juice, brown sugar, salt, and pepper. Cook until bubbly and thick, stirring constantly. Add grapes; heat through. To serve, spoon sauce over squash.

Hominy au Gratin

Makes 4 to 5 servings

 1 can (29 ounces) white hominy, drained
 ¼ cup chopped onion
 1 jar (2 ounces) pimiento, chopped and drained
 2 tablespoons butter *or* margarine, melted
 2 tablespoons flour
 1 teaspoon salt
 1 cup milk
 1 cup grated process American *or* Cheddar cheese

In a greased 1½-quart casserole, combine hominy, onion, and pimiento. In a saucepan, melt butter. Add flour and salt; blend well. Gradually add milk, stirring constantly. Cook until thick and bubbly, stirring constantly. Add cheese; stir until cheese melts. Pour sauce over hominy. Bake at 350° F. 20 minutes or until heated through.

Parmesan Stuffed Onions

Makes 4 servings

 4 large onions, peeled
 ½ cup fine dry bread crumbs
 ½ teaspoon salt
 ½ teaspoon crushed leaf thyme
 2 tablespoons grated Parmesan cheese, divided
 2 tablespoons vegetable oil

In a medium saucepan, place onions; cover with water. Bring to boiling; reduce heat. Cover and simmer 10 minutes; drain and cool. Cut a thin slice from top and bottom of each onion. Stand onions in a large skillet. In a small bowl, combine bread crumbs, salt, thyme, and 1 tablespoon of the cheese; blend well. Spoon 2 tablespoons of the crumb mixture on top of each onion. Drizzle oil over crumb mixture. Sprinkle with remaining 1 tablespoon cheese. Pour 1 inch of hot water into skillet. Cover and simmer 25 minutes, basting onions occasionally with pan liquid. Add more water, if needed.

Great Baked Beans

Makes 8 servings

 1 pound dry beans, such as Great Northern or Michigan Northern, sorted and rinsed
 5 cups warm water
 1½ teaspoons dry mustard
 2 teaspoons salt
 ½ cup plus 2 tablespoons packed brown sugar
 2 tablespoons dark molasses
 ½ pound salt pork, cut in 1-inch pieces
 ½ pound boneless pork shoulder, cut in 1-inch pieces
 1 large onion, quartered

Soak beans in water overnight; drain; reserve soaking liquid. Place beans in a crockpot. In a separate bowl, combine mustard, salt, brown sugar, and molasses. Stir in 5 cups reserved soaking liquid. Pour over beans. Add salt pork, pork shoulder, and onions. Bring to boiling; reduce heat. Simmer 10 to 12 hours, stirring occasionally. Add more water if beans become too dry during cooking.

Green Beans with Sour Cream Sauce

Vegetables

Baked Tomatoes Stuffed with Vegetables

Makes 4 servings

- 4 medium tomatoes
- 2 tablespoons butter or margarine, divided
- 1 cup diced unpeeled eggplant
- ¼ cup sliced carrot
- ¼ cup diced green pepper
- ¼ cup sliced mushrooms
- 2 tablespoons chopped onion
- 1 clove garlic, crushed
- 2 tablespoons minced fresh dillweed or
  2 teaspoons dried
- ¼ teaspoon crushed leaf oregano
- ¼ teaspoon salt
- ⅛ teaspoon black pepper

Cut a ¼-inch-thick slice from the stem end of each tomato. Use a spoon to carefully scoop out pulp; reserve pulp (about 1½ cups). Arrange tomatoes in an 8-inch baking pan; set aside. In a medium skillet, melt 1 tablespoon of the butter. Add eggplant, carrot, green pepper, mushrooms, onion, garlic, and reserved tomato pulp. Sauté about 5 minutes or until vegetables are tender and most of the liquid has evaporated. Stir in dillweed, oregano, salt, and pepper. Fill tomatoes with vegetable mixture, mounding slightly in centers. Dot with remaining 1 tablespoon butter. Pour hot water into the baking pan to a depth of ½ inch. Cover with aluminum foil. Bake at 350° F. 30 minutes or until tomatoes are tender. Use a slotted spoon to remove tomatoes from baking pan to a serving platter.

Puffy Corn Fritters

Makes 16 to 20 fritters

- 1⅓ cups flour
- 1½ teaspoons baking powder
- ¾ teaspoon salt
- 1 tablespoon sugar
- ⅔ cup milk
- 1 egg
- 1 can (17 ounces) whole kernel corn, drained
  Maple syrup

Sift flour, baking powder, salt, and sugar into a large bowl. In a small bowl, combine milk and egg; blend well. Gradually add to dry ingredients; blend well. Add corn; blend well. Heat oil for deep frying to 375° F. Drop batter by tablespoonfuls into hot oil. Deep fry 4 to 8 minutes or until golden. Drain on paper towels. Serve with maple syrup.

Potato Logs

Makes 6 servings

- 2 teaspoons water
- 1 teaspoon instant minced onion
- ½ cup dairy sour cream or plain yogurt
- 4 tablespoons butter or margarine, divided
- 1 tablespoon chopped parsley
- ½ teaspoon salt
- ⅛ teaspoon dried dillweed
  Dash black pepper
- 1½ cups soft bread crumbs
- ¼ cup grated Parmesan cheese
- ⅛ teaspoon paprika
- 6 medium potatoes, cooked and mashed

Grease a 13 x 9-inch baking dish; set aside. In a small bowl, combine water and onion; let stand 10 minutes. Add yogurt, 2 tablespoons of the butter, parsley, and seasonings; blend well. In a small saucepan, melt remaining 2 tablespoons butter. Add bread crumbs, cheese, and paprika; blend well. Using ¼ cup of the mashed potatoes at a time, shape into 4-inch logs. Roll logs in crumb mixture. Place in prepared baking dish. Bake at 400° F. 30 minutes or until golden.

Southern-Style Stuffed Peppers

Makes 4 servings

- 2 tablespoons vegetable oil, divided
- ¾ cup chopped onions, divided
- 2 cloves garlic, crushed
- 1 pound tomatoes, chopped
- ½ cup water
- 1 teaspoon crushed leaf basil
- 2 large green peppers
- 1 cup sliced okra, optional
- 1 cup whole kernel corn
- ¼ teaspoon salt
- ⅛ teaspoon black pepper
- 1 tablespoon butter or margarine

In a medium saucepan, heat 1 tablespoon of the oil. Add ¼ cup of the onions and the garlic; sauté 1 minute. Add tomatoes, water, and basil. Bring to boiling; reduce heat. Cover and simmer 20 minutes. Pour tomato mixture into an 8-inch square baking pan. Cut each pepper lengthwise in half; remove seeds. Arrange peppers in baking pan, cut sides up. In a small saucepan, heat remaining 1 tablespoon oil. Add remaining ½ cup onion; sauté 1 minute. Add okra, corn, salt and black pepper; cook and stir for 5 minutes. Fill peppers with vegetable mixture. Dot with butter. Cover and bake at 350° F. 30 minutes or until peppers are tender.

Creamy German Potato Salad

Makes 8 servings

    1 can (10¾ ounces) cream of celery soup, undiluted
    2 tablespoons lemon juice
    ¼ cup water
    4 medium potatoes, peeled, cooked, and cubed
    ½ cup sliced celery
    ¼ cup chopped parsley
    2 teaspoons salt
    ½ teaspoon sugar
      Dash black pepper
    1 tablespoon crumbled crisp-cooked bacon

In a large saucepan, combine soup, lemon juice, and water. Heat over low heat, stirring occasionally, until blended. Stir in potatoes, celery, parsley, salt, sugar, and pepper; heat through, stirring gently. Serve topped with crumbled bacon.

Creamy Rice Salad

Makes 10 servings

    5 cups cooked rice
    1½ cups diced tomatoes
    1 cup diced green pepper
    ¼ cup finely chopped onion
    ¼ cup chopped parsley
    1 can (10¾ ounces) creamy chicken mushroom soup, undiluted
    ⅓ cup wine vinegar
    3 tablespoons olive or vegetable oil
    1 clove garlic, minced
      Lettuce leaves

In a large bowl, combine rice, tomatoes, green pepper, onion, and parsley; toss lightly to mix. In the container of an electric blender or food processor, combine soup, vinegar, oil, and garlic; blend until smooth. Drizzle over rice mixture; toss lightly. Cover and refrigerate at least 4 hours. Serve on lettuce leaves.

Caesar Potato Salad

Makes 8 servings

    1 egg
    ¼ cup Italian dressing
    ¼ cup grated romano cheese
    1 tablespoon Worcestershire sauce
    2 teaspoons prepared mustard
    1 teaspoon salt
    4 medium potatoes, peeled, cooked, and cubed
    4 pitted ripe olives, sliced

In a large bowl, combine egg, Italian dressing, cheese, Worcestershire sauce, mustard, and salt; beat with a wire whisk until well blended. Add potatoes and olives; toss lightly to mix. Chill well before serving.

Garden Potato Salad

Makes 8 servings

    ¼ cup low-fat plain yogurt
    ¼ cup cottage cheese
    2 teaspoons milk
    ½ teaspoon cider vinegar
    ½ teaspoon onion powder
    ¼ teaspoon crushed leaf tarragon
    ¼ teaspoon salt
      Dash black pepper
    2 pounds new potatoes
    1 cup cut green beans
    ½ cup fresh corn kernels or canned corn
    ½ cup shredded carrot

In an electric blender or food processor, combine yogurt, cottage cheese, milk, vinegar, onion powder, tarragon, salt, and pepper; blend until smooth; set aside. Cook potatoes in boiling salted water about 15 minutes or until tender. Drain; cut in quarters. Place potatoes in a large bowl. Cook beans in 1 inch boiling water 2 to 3 minutes or until tender-crisp; drain well. Add beans, corn, and carrot to potatoes. Pour on salad dressing; mix lightly. Cover and refrigerate at least 2 hours before serving.

Ambrosia Fruit Salad

Makes 10 to 12 servings

    1 can (14 ounces) sweetened condensed milk
    1 carton (8 ounces) plain yogurt
    ½ cup lime juice
    2 cans (11 ounces each) mandarin orange segments, drained; reserve 8 for garnish
    1 can (20 ounces) pineapple chunks, drained
    1½ cups grape halves, seeded, if necessary
    1 can (3½ ounces) flaked coconut (1⅓ cups)
    1 cup miniature marshmallows
    1 cup chopped pecans or walnuts
    ½ cup sliced maraschino cherries, drained

In a large bowl, combine sweetened condensed milk, yogurt, and lime juice; blend well. Stir in remaining ingredients. Chill at least 2 hours to blend flavors. Serve on lettuce leaves, if desired. Garnish with reserved orange segments.

Salads and Fruit

Nectarine and Pasta Salad

Makes 8 servings

- ½ cup vegetable oil
- ½ cup white wine vinegar
- 3 tablespoons minced chives
- 1½ teaspoons salt
- 1½ teaspoons dry mustard
- 1 teaspoon crushed leaf summer savory
- ½ teaspoon black pepper
- 3 cups julienne-cut cooked pork
- 3 cups cooked rotelle, shells *or* elbow macaroni
- 1 pound nectarines, sliced (about 4)
- 1 small cucumber, sliced
  Lettuce leaves

In a large bowl, combine oil, vinegar, chives, salt, mustard, savory, and pepper; blend well with a wire whisk. Add pork, pasta, nectarines, and cucumber; toss gently. Cover and chill about 1 hour to blend flavors, stirring occasionally. Serve on individual plates lined with lettuce leaves.

Shrimp and Mushroom Salad with Pecan Dressing

Makes 4 servings

- ¾ pound fresh *or* thawed frozen shrimp, cooked, peeled, and deveined
- 2 cups sliced mushrooms
- 1 cup cubed Gruyere cheese
- ¼ cup chopped parsley
- 3 tablespoons olive *or* vegetable oil
- ½ teaspoon salt
- ¼ teaspoon black pepper
  Lettuce leaves
  Pecan Dressing (recipe follows)

In a 2-quart mixing bowl, combine shrimp, mushrooms, cheese, parsley, olive oil, salt, and pepper; toss lightly to mix. Arrange on a lettuce-lined platter. Serve with Pecan Dressing.

Pecan Dressing

Makes about ½ cup

- ½ cup broken pecans
- ¼ cup water
- 1 clove garlic
- 4 teaspoons white wine vinegar
- ¼ teaspoon salt
- ⅛ teaspoon cayenne pepper

In an electric blender or food processor, combine all ingredients. Blend until pecans are finely chopped.

Spinach and Orange Salad

Makes 4 to 6 servings

- ½ pound fresh spinach, rinsed, stems removed, and patted dry
- 1 bunch romaine
- 2 oranges
- 1 sweet red onion, thinly sliced
- ⅛ cup olive oil
- ⅛ cup vegetable oil
- ¼ cup fresh orange juice
- 2 tablespoons wine vinegar
- 1 teaspoon salt
- ⅛ teaspoon black pepper
- ½ teaspoon paprika

Tear spinach and romaine into bite-size pieces. Place in a large salad bowl. Peel oranges; cut into thin slices. Add oranges and onion to lettuce; toss lightly to mix. In a small bowl, combine olive and vegetable oils, orange juice, vinegar, salt, pepper, and paprika; blend well. Before serving, drizzle dressing over salad; toss lightly.

Tart Citrus Salad

Makes 4 servings

- 1 can (15 ounces) artichoke hearts
- ¼ cup vegetable oil
- 2 tablespoons vinegar
- 1 teaspoon Worcestershire sauce
- ½ teaspoon salt
- ⅛ teaspoon black pepper
  Dash paprika
- 2 pink or white grapefruit
- 4 cups mixed salad greens

Drain artichoke hearts; cut in halves. In a small bowl, mix oil, vinegar, Worcestershire sauce, salt, pepper, and paprika. Add artichokes; blend well. Cover and chill several hours. When ready to serve, peel and section grapefruit. In a salad bowl, combine salad greens, artichoke mixture, and grapefruit; toss lightly to mix.

Salads and Fruit

Last Minute Salad with Yogurt Dressing

Makes 4 servings

- ¾ cup plain yogurt
- 1 teaspoon prepared mustard
- ¾ teaspoon dillweed
- ⅛ teaspoon salt
- ⅛ teaspoon black pepper
- 2 cups shredded iceberg lettuce
- ½ cup sliced celery
- ½ cup sliced cucumber
- ¼ cup sliced radishes

In a small bowl, combine yogurt, mustard, dillweed, salt, and pepper; blend well. Let stand at least 15 minutes to blend flavors. In a large salad bowl, combine lettuce, celery, cucumber, and radishes; toss lightly. Just before serving, drizzle on just enough dressing to coat vegetables completely. Refrigerate remaining dressing for later use.

Golden Fruit Compote

Makes 6 servings

- 1 can (8 ounces) water-pack apricot halves, drained
- 1 can (8 ounces) pineapple chunks, packed in unsweetened juice; reserve liquid
- 2 tablespoons raisins
- ½ tablespoon lemon juice
- 1 cinnamon stick
- 2 whole cloves
- 1 Golden Delicious apple, cored and sliced

In a large saucepan, combine apricots, pineapple and juice, raisins, lemon juice, cinnamon, and cloves. Bring to boiling; reduce heat. Cover and simmer 15 minutes or until heated through. Add apples. Cook 5 minutes or until apples are tender but firm. Serve warm in individual fruit cups.

Grape Cup

Makes 4 servings

- ¼ cup orange juice
- 2 tablespoons orange liqueur or orange juice
- ½ cup seedless grapes
- ½ cup red or blue-black grapes, seeded
- ½ cup grapefruit segments
- ½ cup cubed melon
- ½ cup sliced banana
- 4 small grape clusters

In a bowl, combine orange juice and liqueur. Stir in all fruit, except grape clusters. Chill well. To serve, divide among 4 fruit cups and garnish each serving with a small cluster of grapes.

Vegetable Medley with Onion Dressing

Makes 8 servings

- Onion Dressing (recipe follows)
- 1 cup soft bread crumbs
- 2 cups green pepper strips
- 3 cups shredded cabbage
- 2 cups sliced and halved cucumbers
- 4 cups cut-up tomatoes
- 1 cup diced celery

Prepare Onion Dressing; set aside. In a large, straight-sided salad dish, layer half the bread crumbs, green peppers, cabbage, cucumbers, tomatoes, celery, and Onion Dressing. Repeat layers with remaining half of ingredients. Cover and refrigerate several hours or overnight.

Onion Dressing

Makes about 1 cup

- ½ cup chopped onion
- 2 teaspoons minced garlic
- 2 teaspoons Dijon mustard
- 1 teaspoon grated lemon peel
- 1 teaspoon salt
- ¼ teaspoon crushed leaf oregano
- ¼ teaspoon black pepper
- ¼ cup lemon juice
- ¾ cup vegetable oil

In an electric blender or food processor, combine onion, garlic, mustard, lemon peel, salt, oregano, pepper, and lemon juice; blend until smooth. With machine running, very slowly drizzle in oil until all oil is blended into dressing.

Brunch Compote

Makes 6 to 8 servings

- 1 cup canned apricot halves, drained
- 3 tablespoons sugar
- 3 tablespoons orange or pineapple juice
- 3 Bartlett pears, peeled, cored, and cut in wedges
- 2 oranges, peeled and sliced
- 1 small cantaloupe, cut in chunks
- ½ pound grapes, halved; seeded, if necessary

In an electric blender or food processor, puree apricots. In a small saucepan, combine pureed apricots and sugar; heat until sugar dissolves, stirring constantly. Stir in orange juice. Chill well. In a large bowl, combine pears, oranges, cantaloupe, and grapes. Pour apricot sauce over fruit; toss lightly to coat fruit. Serve in individual fruit cups.

Citrus Fruit Bowl

Makes 6 servings

- 1 jar (32 ounces) chilled unsweetened grapefruit sections
- 1 cup cranberry-orange sauce
- 2 medium bananas

Drain grapefruit sections; reserve ¾ cup juice. In a bowl, combine grapefruit sections, cranberry-orange sauce, and reserved juice. Chill. Just before serving, slice bananas; stir into grapefruit mixture.

Champagne Fruit Salad

Makes 4 to 6 servings

- 1 envelope unflavored gelatin
- 1 cup apple juice
- 3 tablespoons sugar
- 1 cup champagne *or* ginger ale
- 2 cups grapes, seeded, if necessary, and halved
- 1 orange, peeled and broken into segments
- ⅓ cup broken pecans
  Lettuce leaves

In a small saucepan, soften gelatin in apple juice. Heat to dissolve gelatin, stirring constantly. Add sugar; stir until dissolved. Stir in champagne. Chill until partially set. Stir in grapes, orange segments, and pecans. Pour into a lightly oiled 4-cup ring mold. Chill until firm. Unmold onto a lettuce-lined platter.

Holiday Fruit Bowl

Makes 6 servings

- ¾ cup orange juice
- 2 tablespoons lime juice
- ¼ cup sugar
- 1 teaspoon grated orange peel
  Dash salt
- 3 oranges, peeled and sectioned
- 2 tangerines *or* tangelos, peeled and sectioned
- 2 grapefruit, peeled and sectioned
- 1 cup walnut halves

In a saucepan, combine orange juice, lime juice, sugar, orange peel, and salt. Bring to boiling; boil 1 minute. Remove from heat. Let stand until cool. In a medium bowl, combine orange, tangerine, and grapefruit sections; pour syrup over fruit. Cover and chill 1 hour. Before serving, sprinkle nuts on top.

Lemony Poached Golden Apples

Makes 6 servings

- 3 Golden Delicious apples
- 1½ cups apple juice
  Peel of ½ lemon
- ⅛ teaspoon ground ginger

Core apples; remove peel around top half of each. In a saucepan, combine apple juice, lemon peel, and ginger. Bring to boiling; reduce heat. Simmer, uncovered, 5 minutes. Place apples in hot apple juice. Cover and simmer about 15 minutes or until apples are tender but still hold their shape, basting and rotating apples frequently. Remove apples from pan with a slotted spoon. Cut each apple in half. Place halves in individual serving dishes. Strain juice and return to pan. Cook, uncovered, until juice is reduced to 1 cup. Serve warm over warm apples.

Summer Fruit Salad

Makes 6 to 8 servings

- 1 cantaloupe, cubed
- 1 honeydew melon, cubed
- ⅓ whole watermelon, cut in chunks
- 4 bananas, sliced
- 4 oranges, peeled and sliced
- 1½ pints strawberries, cleaned and hulled
  Sugar
- 2 bottles (7 ounces each) pineapple *or* lemon juice *or* ginger ale

In a large bowl, combine cantaloupe, melons, bananas, oranges, and strawberries; toss lightly to mix. Add sugar to sweeten as needed. Pour pineapple juice over fruit. Chill well before serving.

Sautéed Apples

Makes 6 servings

- 2 tablespoons butter *or* margarine
- 3 red cooking apples, quartered, cored, and sliced
- 2 tablespoons brown sugar
- 1 tablespoon lemon juice
- ¼ teaspoon ground cinnamon

In a large skillet, melt butter. Add apples, lemon juice, and cinnamon; sauté until just tender, stirring gently.

Lime Plum Mold

Makes 6 to 8 servings

     1 package (3 ounces) lime-flavored gelatin
     1 cup boiling water
    ¾ cup cold water
     3 or 4 whole prune plums, cut in quarters
    ½ cup whipping cream, whipped
    1½ cups sliced prune plums
     1 cup miniature marshmallows
    ½ cup chopped pecans
       Lettuce leaves

In a small bowl, dissolve gelatin in boiling water. Stir in cold water. Arrange quartered plums in the bottom of a lightly oiled 6-cup mold. Add just enough gelatin to hold plums in place. Chill until firm. Chill remaining gelatin until partially set. Beat with an electric mixer until fluffy. Fold in whipped cream, sliced plums, marshmallows, and pecans. Pour into prepared mold. Chill until firm. Unmold onto a lettuce-lined platter.

Apricot Cheese Mold

Makes 8 servings

     1 package (3 ounces) lemon-flavored gelatin
     1 cup boiling water
     1 can apricots, drained and sliced; reserve 1 cup juice
       (add water, if necessary, to equal one cup)
     1 carton (12 ounces) cottage cheese
     1 cup whipping cream, whipped
    ½ cup coarsely chopped walnuts
    ½ cup maraschino cherries, quartered
       Sliced canned apricots, optional

In a small bowl, dissolve gelatin in boiling water. Stir in reserved apricot juice. Chill until partially set. Stir in cottage cheese. Fold in whipped cream, nuts, cherries, and apricots. Pour into a lightly oiled 1½-quart mold. Chill until firm. Garnish with additional apricot slices, if desired.

Strawberry Pineapple Salad

Makes 4 servings

     1 package (8 ounces) cream cheese, softened
     3 tablespoons honey
     2 cups strawberries, hulled and crushed
     1 cup crushed pineapple, drained
       Lettuce leaves
       Sliced strawberries, optional

In a bowl, combine cream cheese and honey; blend well. Add strawberries and pineapple; blend well. Pour into a freezer tray; freeze 2 hours. Cut into 4 portions. Serve on lettuce leaves. Garnish with sliced strawberries, if desired.

Garden Salad Mold

Makes 4 to 6 servings

     1 package (3 ounces) lemon-flavored gelatin
    ½ teaspoon salt
     1 cup boiling water
     1 cup milk
    ½ cup mayonnaise or salad dressing
     2 tablespoons vinegar
    ½ cup chopped celery
    ½ cup shredded cabbage
    ½ cup shredded carrot
     2 tablespoons chopped green pepper
     1 tablespoon minced onion
       Lettuce leaves

In a small bowl, dissolve gelatin and salt in boiling water; let stand until cool. In a separate bowl, combine milk, mayonnaise, and vinegar; blend well. Gradually add gelatin mixture to milk mixture; blend well. Chill until partially set. Stir in celery, cabbage, carrot, green pepper, and onion. Pour into a lightly oiled 4-cup mold. Chill until firm. Unmold onto a lettuce-lined serving platter.

Frosty Cheese Mold

Makes 6 servings

     1 envelope unflavored gelatin
    ¼ cup water
     1 cup milk, divided
    1½ cups cottage cheese
    ¼ cup crumbled blue cheese
     1 can (6 ounces) frozen limeade concentrate, thawed
    ½ cup chopped pecans
    ½ cup whipping cream, whipped
       Salad greens, optional
       Fresh fruit, optional

In a small saucepan, sprinkle gelatin over water; let stand to soften. Stir in ½ cup milk. Heat over low heat until gelatin dissolves, stirring constantly. Stir in remaining ½ cup milk. In a small mixing bowl, beat cheeses with an electric mixer until fairly smooth. Stir in gelatin mixture and limeade. Chill until partially set. Fold in pecans and whipped cream. Pour into a lightly oiled 4½-cup ring mold. Chill until firm. Unmold onto salad greens and serve with fresh fruit, if desired.

Strawberry Pineapple Salad

Breads and Breakfasts

Pumpkin Bread

Makes 2 loaves

- 3 cups sugar
- 1 cup vegetable oil
- 4 eggs, lightly beaten
- 2 cups canned pumpkin
- 3½ cups flour
- 2 teaspoons baking soda
- 1 teaspoon baking powder
- 1 teaspoon salt
- 1 teaspoon nutmeg
- 1 teaspoon ground allspice
- 1 teaspoon ground cinnamon
- ½ teaspoon ground cloves
- ⅔ cup water

Grease a 9 x 5-inch loaf pan; set aside. Preheat oven to 350° F. In a large mixing bowl, combine sugar, oil, eggs, and pumpkin; blend well. In a separate bowl, combine flour, baking soda, baking powder, salt, nutmeg, allspice, cinnamon, and cloves. Alternately add flour mixture and water to pumpkin mixture, beginning and ending with flour; blend well after each addition. Pour batter into prepared pans. Bake 1½ hours or until a wooden pick inserted in the center comes out clean. Cool in pans 10 minutes. Invert onto a wire rack to cool completely.

Carrot Bread

Makes 1 loaf

- ¾ cup vegetable oil
- 1 cup sugar
- 2 eggs
- 1½ cups flour
- ¼ teaspoon salt
- 1 teaspoon baking soda
- 1 teaspoon ground cinnamon
- 1 cup grated carrots
- 1 cup chopped dates
- 1 cup chopped nuts

Grease an 8 x 4-inch loaf pan; set aside. Preheat oven to 350° F. In a large mixing bowl, combine oil, sugar, and eggs; blend well. In a separate bowl, combine flour, salt, baking soda, and cinnamon. Alternately add flour mixture and carrots to mixing bowl; blend well after each addition. Stir in dates and nuts. Pour batter into prepared pan. Bake 1 hour or until a wooden pick inserted in the center comes out clean. Cool in pan 10 minutes. Invert onto a wire rack to cool completely.

Chocolate Zucchini Bread

Makes 2 loaves

- 3 eggs
- 1 cup vegetable oil
- 2 cups sugar
- 2 cups grated zucchini (Do not drain)
- 3 cups flour
- ½ teaspoon baking powder
- 1 teaspoon salt
- 1 teaspoon baking soda
- 1 tablespoon ground cinnamon
- ¼ teaspoon ground cloves
- ¼ teaspoon ground allspice
- ¼ cup unsweetened cocoa
- ½ cup chopped nuts
- 1 tablespoon vanilla

Grease two 9 x 5-inch loaf pans; set aside. Preheat oven to 350° F. In a large mixing bowl, combine eggs, oil, and sugar; beat until well blended. Add zucchini along with liquid; blend well. In a separate bowl, sift together flour, baking powder, salt, baking soda, cinnamon, cloves, allspice, and cocoa. Gradually add to zucchini mixture; blend well. Beat in vanilla. Stir in nuts. Pour batter into prepared pans. Bake 1 hour or until a wooden pick inserted in the center comes out clean. Cool in pans 10 minutes. Invert onto a wire rack to cool completely.

Applesauce Nut Bread

Makes 1 loaf

- 2 cups flour
- ¾ cup sugar
- 1 tablespoon baking powder
- 1 teaspoon salt
- ½ teaspoon baking soda
- ½ teaspoon ground cinnamon
- 1 egg, lightly beaten
- 1 cup applesauce
- 2 tablespoons vegetable shortening, melted
- 1 cup chopped nuts

Grease an 8 x 4-inch loaf pan; set aside. Preheat oven to 350° F. In a bowl, sift together flour, sugar, baking powder, salt, baking soda, and cinnamon; set aside. In a mixing bowl, combine egg, applesauce, and melted shortening; blend well. Gradually add flour mixture; blend well. Stir in nuts. Turn batter into prepared pan. Bake 1 hour or until a wooden pick inserted in the center comes out clean. Cool in pan 10 minutes. Invert onto a wire rack to cool completely.

Apricot Bread

Makes 1 loaf

- 2 cups flour
- 1 cup sugar
- 2½ teaspoons baking powder
- ¾ teaspoon salt
- ¾ cup crunchy nut-like cereal
- ⅔ cup chopped dried apricots
- 1 egg
- 1¼ cups milk
- 2 tablespoons vegetable shortening, melted

Grease a 9 x 5-inch loaf pan; set aside. Preheat oven to 350° F. In a large bowl, combine flour, sugar, baking powder, and salt. Stir in cereal and apricots. In a small bowl, beat egg and milk together. Stir in melted shortening. Add liquids to flour mixture; stir until evenly moist. Turn batter into prepared pan. Bake at 1 hour or until a wooden pick inserted in the center comes out clean. Cool in pan 10 minutes. Invert onto a wire rack to cool completely.

Popovers

Makes 6 servings

- 3 eggs
- 1 cup flour
- ½ teaspoon salt
- 1 cup milk

Preheat oven to 450° F. Generously grease popover pans or large muffin cups. In a small bowl, beat eggs lightly. Add flour, salt, and milk; mix until just blended. Do not overbeat. Fill prepared pans ½ full with batter. Bake at 450° F. 15 minutes; reduce oven temperature to 325° F. Bake 25 to 30 minutes or until deep golden brown.

Poppy Seed Muffins

Makes about 16

- ¾ cup sugar
- ¼ cup butter or margarine, softened
- ½ teaspoon grated orange peel
- 2 eggs
- 2 cups flour
- 2½ teaspoons baking powder
- ½ teaspoon salt
- ¼ teaspoon ground nutmeg
- 1 cup milk
- ½ cup golden raisins
- ½ cup chopped pecans
- ¼ cup poppy seed

In a large mixing bowl, cream sugar, butter, and orange peel with an electric mixer until light and fluffy. Add eggs, one at a time, beating well after each addition. In a separate bowl, combine flour, baking powder, salt, and nutmeg. Alternately add flour mixture and milk to creamed mixture; blend well after each addition. Stir in raisins, nuts, and poppy seed. Fill paper-lined muffin cups ¾ full with batter. Bake at 400° F. 20 minutes or until golden.

Bran Muffins

Makes 6 dozen

- 2 cups boiling water
- 2 cups bran
- 3 scant cups sugar
- 1 cup vegetable shortening
- 4 eggs, lightly beaten
- 1 quart buttermilk
- 5 cups flour
- 5 teaspoons baking soda
- ½ teaspoon salt
- 4 cups coarsely crushed bran cereal

In a bowl, pour boiling water over bran; let stand 5 minutes. In a mixing bowl, cream sugar and shortening until light and fluffy. Add eggs, buttermilk, and bran mixture; blend well. In a separate bowl, combine flour, baking soda, salt, and bran cereal. Gradually add to liquid mixture, blending well after each addition. Fill greased muffin cups about ⅔ full with batter. Bake at 400° F. 15 to 20 minutes or until golden. Can be stored in refrigerator up to 5 weeks.

Cranberry Orange Muffins

Makes about 12

- 2 cups flour
- ½ teaspoon salt
- 1½ teaspoons baking powder
- ½ teaspoon baking soda
- ¼ cup sugar
- ⅔ cup boiling water
- 2 tablespoons butter or margarine
- 1 cup cranberry relish
- 1 tablespoon grated orange peel
- 1 egg, lightly beaten

Into a large bowl, sift together flour, salt, baking powder, baking soda, and sugar. Stir butter into boiling water. Cool to room temperature. Stir egg into water. Gradually add liquids to dry ingredients; blend well. Stir in cranberry relish and orange peel. Fill greased muffin cups ⅔ full with batter. Bake at 425° F. 40 to 45 minutes or until golden.

Dilly Bread
Makes 1 loaf

2½ to 3 cups flour, divided
2 tablespoons sugar
2 to 3 teaspoons instant minced onion
2 teaspoons dill seed
1¼ teaspoons salt
¼ teaspoon baking soda
1 package (¼ ounce) active dry yeast
1 carton (8 ounces) cream-style cottage cheese
¼ cup lukewarm water (110 to 115° F.)
1 tablespoon butter or margarine
1 egg
Butter, softened

In a large mixing bowl, combine 1 cup flour, sugar, onion, dill seed, salt, baking soda, and yeast; set aside. In a saucepan, heat cottage cheese, water, and butter until very warm (120 to 130° F.). Add warm liquid and egg to flour mixture; blend on low speed of electric mixer until moistened, then beat 3 minutes at medium speed. Stir in remaining 1½ to 2 cups flour by hand to form a stiff batter. Place in a greased bowl; lightly oil top. Cover and let rise in warm, draft-free place until doubled in bulk, 45 to 65 minutes. Punch down. Turn dough into a well-greased 1½- or 2-quart casserole. Cover and let rise until doubled in bulk, 30 to 45 minutes. Preheat oven to 350° F. Bake 35 to 40 minutes or until golden. Turn out of casserole onto a wire rack to cool. Brush bread with butter while still warm.

Pecan Rolls
Makes 1 dozen

½ cup milk
4 tablespoons butter or margarine
⅓ cup granulated sugar
½ teaspoon salt
1 egg, lightly beaten
¼ cup lukewarm water (105 to 115° F.)
1 package (¼ ounce) active dry yeast
1 teaspoon granulated sugar
2½ to 3 cups flour, divided
3 tablespoons butter, melted
1 teaspoon ground cinnamon
6 tablespoons granulated sugar
½ cup packed brown sugar
1 cup chopped pecans

In a saucepan, scald milk. Add 4 tablespoons butter, ⅓ cup sugar, and salt; stir until butter melts. Cool to room temperature. Stir in egg; set aside. In a measuring cup, sprinkle yeast and 1 teaspoon sugar over water; let stand 5 minutes to dissolve yeast. In a large mixing bowl, combine milk and yeast mixtures. Stir in 1 cup of the flour to make a soft batter. Gradually stir in remaining flour to make a stiff dough. Turn dough out onto a lightly floured surface. Knead until smooth and elastic, 8 to 10 minutes. Place dough in a greased bowl; turn to grease top. Cover and let rise in a warm, draft-free place until doubled in bulk, about 1½ hours. Roll dough out into a 16 x 8-inch rectangle. Brush top with 3 tablespoons melted butter. In a small bowl, combine cinnamon and brown sugar. Sprinkle cinnamon mixture over dough. Roll up tightly from the long side. Cut into 12 pieces. Generously grease a 12-cup muffin pan. Sprinkle ½ cup brown sugar in muffin cups. Divide pecans among muffin cups. Place a piece of dough, cut side down, in each muffin cup. Cover and let rise 30 minutes. Preheat oven to 375° F. Bake 15 minutes or until golden. Turn rolls out onto a wire rack to cool.

Sesame Twist
Makes 2 loaves

5½ to 6 cups flour, divided
2 packages (¼ ounce each) active dry yeast
1 cup milk
1 cup water
2 tablespoons sugar
2 tablespoons vegetable oil
2 teaspoons salt
1 egg white beaten with 1 tablespoon water
Sesame seed

In a large bowl, stir together 2 cups flour and yeast. In a saucepan, combine milk, water, sugar, 2 tablespoons oil, and salt; heat over low heat until very warm (120 to 130° F.) Stir liquids into flour mixture. Beat on high speed of an electric mixer 3 minutes or until smooth. Stir in enough remaining flour to make a soft dough. Turn dough out onto a lightly floured surface. Knead until smooth and elastic, 8 to 10 minutes. Cover and let rise 20 minutes. Divide dough in 4 parts. Roll each part into a 15-inch rope. Spiral-wrap 2 ropes; tuck ends under. Repeat. Place in two greased 8 x 4-inch loaf pans. Brush tops with egg white mixture. Sprinkle with sesame seed. Cover and let rise in a warm draft-free place until doubled in bulk, 30 to 45 minutes. Preheat oven to 400° F. Bake 35 to 40 minutes or until loaves sound hollow when lightly tapped. Turn out of pans onto a wire rack to cool.

Breads and Breakfasts

Quick Orange Coffee Cake

Makes 10 servings

- ⅔ cup sugar
- 1 tablespoon grated orange peel
- 2 packages (10 ounces each) refrigerated buttermilk biscuits
- 3 tablespoons butter *or* margarine, melted
- ½ cup powdered sugar
- 1 tablespoon orange juice

Grease a 9-inch round baking pan; set aside. Preheat oven to 375° F. In a small bowl, combine sugar and orange peel. Separate biscuits. Dip each into melted butter, then into sugar mixture to coat well. In prepared pan, arrange dough in 4 rows of 5 biscuits each, overlapping slightly. Sprinkle any remaining sugar mixture on top. Bake 35 minutes or until golden. Cool on a wire rack 10 minutes. Turn out onto a serving plate. In a small bowl, combine powdered sugar and orange juice; blend well. Drizzle over coffee cake.

Orange Glazed Coffee Cake

Makes 1 large coffee cake

- 1 package (¼ ounce) active dry yeast
- ¼ cup lukewarm water (110 to 115° F.)
- ¼ cup sugar
- 1 teaspoon salt
- ½ cup dairy sour cream
- ½ cup butter *or* margarine, melted, divided
- 2 eggs
- 2¾ to 3 cups flour, divided
  Coconut Filling (recipe follows)
  Orange Glaze (recipe follows)
- ¼ cup flaked coconut

In a mixing bowl, sprinkle yeast over water. Let stand 5 minutes to dissolve yeast. Stir in sugar, salt, sour cream, 6 tablespoons butter, and eggs. Add 1¾ cups flour; beat 2 minutes on medium speed of an electric mixer. Stir in remaining 1 to 1¼ cups flour to make a soft dough. Cover and let rise in a warm, draft-free place until doubled in bulk, 45 to 60 minutes. In a small bowl, prepare Coconut Filling; set aside. Turn dough out onto a floured surface. Knead about 15 times. Roll out half of the dough into a 12-inch circle. Brush with 1 tablespoon melted butter. Sprinkle with half of the Coconut Filling. Cut into 12 wedges. Roll up each wedge, starting from the wide end. Repeat with remaining half of dough and Coconut Filling. Place rolls, seam sides down, in a greased 13 x 9-inch baking pan. Cover and let rise in a warm, draft-free place until doubled in bulk. Pre-

heat oven to 350° F. Bake 45 to 60 minutes or until golden brown. Place pan on a wire rack to cool. Prepare Orange Glaze. Pour glaze over hot coffee cake. Sprinkle with coconut.

Coconut Filling

- ¾ cup sugar
- 1 cup coconut, toasted
- 2 tablespoons grated orange peel

In a small bowl, mix all ingredients.

Orange Glaze

- ¾ cup sugar
- ½ cup dairy sour cream
- ¼ cup butter *or* margarine
- 2 tablespoons orange juice

In a small saucepan, mix all ingredients. Bring to boiling; boil 3 minutes, stirring frequently.

Cinnamon Coffee Round

Makes 1 coffee cake

- Streusel Topping (recipe follows)
- ¾ cup sugar
- 6 tablespoons vegetable shortening
- 1 egg
- 2 cups flour
- 2 teaspoons baking powder
- 1 teaspoon salt
- 1 cup milk

Grease an 8-inch round baking pan; set aside. Preheat oven to 350° F. Prepare Streusel Topping; set aside. In a mixing bowl, cream sugar and shortening with an electric mixer until light and fluffy. Beat in egg. In a separate bowl, sift together flour, baking powder, and salt. Alternately add flour mixture and milk to creamed mixture; blend well after each addition. Stir in half of the Streusel Topping. Spread batter into prepared pan. (Can be made ahead to this point and refrigerated overnight, if desired.) Smooth top of dough. Sprinkle with remaining Streusel Topping. Bake 30 to 35 minutes or until a wooden pick inserted in the center comes out clean. Serve warm.

Streusel Topping

- ½ cup sugar
- 2 tablespoons flour
- 1 tablespoon ground cinnamon
- 2 tablespoons butter *or* margarine, melted
- ¾ cup chopped nuts
- ⅓ cup raisins, optional

In a small bowl, combine all ingredients; stir until blended.

Best Raised Doughnuts

Makes about 40

    1 package (¼ ounce) active dry yeast
    ¼ cup lukewarm water (110 to 115° F.)
    6 cups flour
    1 cup packed brown sugar
    1 teaspoon salt
    1 teaspoon ground cinnamon *or* nutmeg
    1 cup milk, scalded and cooled
    2 eggs, lightly beaten
    1 cup butter, softened
      Vegetable oil

Sprinkle yeast over water; let stand 5 minutes to dissolve yeast. Sift together flour, sugar, salt, and cinnamon. In a large bowl, combine milk and yeast. Stir in 1 cup flour mixture. Gradually stir in remaining flour. Stir in eggs. Cover and let rise in a warm, draft-free place until doubled in bulk, about 1 hour. Punch down. Work in butter until well-blended. Roll out dough on a lightly floured surface to ½-inch thickness. Cut out with a doughnut cutter. Place rounds on a waxed paper-lined tray. Cover and let rise until light and puffy. Heat oil for deep frying to 375° F. Deep fry several doughnuts at a time until golden on both sides. Drain on paper towels.

Daisy Petalled Coffee Cake

Makes 1 coffee cake

    1 package (¼ ounce) active dry yeast
    ¼ cup lukewarm water (110 to 115° F.)
    ½ cup milk
    ¼ cup sugar
    1 teaspoon salt
    2 tablespoons butter *or* margarine
    2½ cups flour, divided
    1 egg
    2 tablespoons butter *or* margarine, melted
    ¼ cup sugar
    1½ teaspoons ground cinnamon
    1 cup sifted powdered sugar
    1 to 2 tablespoons hot water

In a large bowl, sprinkle yeast over water; let stand 5 minutes to dissolve yeast. In a saucepan, scald milk. Add sugar, salt, and shortening; let stand until lukewarm. Add 1 cup flour; blend well to make a thick batter. Stir in yeast and egg; blend well. Add enough remaining flour to make a soft dough. Turn dough out onto a floured surface. Knead until smooth and elastic, 8 to 10 minutes. Place in a greased bowl; turn once to grease top. Cover and let rise in a warm, draft-free place until doubled in bulk, 1½ hours. Punch down; let rest 10 minutes. Roll dough out to a ¼-inch-thick square. Brush one half with melted butter. Combine sugar and cinnamon. Sprinkle ⅓ sugar mixture over buttered side of dough. Fold dough in half. Brush with butter. Sprinkle with ⅓ sugar mixture. Repeat once. Roll dough out to a 12-inch circle. Using a scissors or sharp knife, cut dough from outside to within 1 inch of the center to make 16 wedges. Twist each piece 2 or 3 times. Cover and let rise until doubled in bulk, about 45 minutes. Preheat oven to 350° F. Bake about 20 minutes or until golden. Cool in pan on a wire rack. When cool, combine powdered sugar and water. Drizzle over coffee cake.

Blueberry Coffee Cake

Makes 1 coffee cake

    1 egg, lightly beaten
    10 tablespoons sugar, divided
    1¼ cups flour
    2 teaspoons baking powder
    ¾ teaspoon salt
    ½ cup milk
    3 tablespoons butter *or* margarine, melted
    1 cup fresh blueberries
    1 tablespoon butter *or* margarine, melted

In a mixing bowl, blend egg and 8 tablespoons sugar. In a separate bowl, sift together flour, baking powder, and salt. Alternately add flour and milk to egg mixture; beat well after each addition. Stir in 3 tablespoons melted butter. Fold in blueberries. Turn batter into a greased 8-inch square baking pan. Sprinkle with remaining 2 tablespoons sugar. Cover and refrigerate overnight. Preheat oven to 350° F. Bake 35 minutes or until top springs back when lightly touched. Brush top with remaining butter. Cool in pan on a wire rack.

Easy Pineapple Rolls

Makes 10 servings

    1 can (8 ounces) crushed pineapple, drained
    ¼ cup packed brown sugar
    2 tablespoons butter *or* margarine
    1 package (10 ounces) refrigerated flaky
      buttermilk biscuits

In a small saucepan, combine pineapple, brown sugar, and butter. Heat over low heat, stirring constantly, until butter melts and mixture is hot. Spoon 1 tablespoon into each of 10 medium muffin cups. Separate biscuits. Place 1 biscuit in each muffin cup. Preheat oven ot 400° F. Bake 12 minutes or until golden. Loosen biscuits with a knife. Turn out onto a large serving plate.

Breads and Breakfasts

Peachy Waffles

Makes 4 servings

1 can (16 ounces) sliced cling peaches, drained; reserve liquid
¼ cup packed brown sugar
2 teaspoons cornstarch
½ teaspoon maple flavoring
2 tablespoons butter *or* margarine
Waffles (recipe follows)

In a saucepan, combine reserved peach liquid, brown sugar, cornstarch, maple flavoring, and butter; blend well. Cook over low heat, stirring constantly, until boiling; reduce heat. Cook and stir until thick. Add peaches. Serve over warm waffles.

Waffles

Makes 4 waffles

1⅓ cups flour
2 tablespoons sugar
2½ teaspoons baking powder
½ teaspoon salt
2 eggs, separated
1 cup milk
⅓ cup vegetable shortening, melted

In a mixing bowl, combine flour, sugar, baking powder, and salt; blend well. Stir in egg yolks, milk, and shortening; blend well. In a small mixing bowl, beat egg whites with an electric mixer until stiff peaks form. Gently fold into waffle batter. Bake on a preheated waffle iron until golden.

Apple Pancakes

Makes 4 servings

2 cups flour
4 teaspoons baking powder
1 tablespoon sugar
1 teaspoon salt
½ teaspoon ground cinnamon
2 eggs, lightly beaten
1½ cups milk
¼ cup butter *or* margarine, melted
1 apple, peeled, cored, and chopped

In a large bowl, sift together flour, baking powder, sugar, salt, and cinnamon. In a separate bowl, combine eggs, milk, and butter. Add egg mixture to flour mixture; stir just until flour is moistened. Stir in chopped apple. Drop batter by ¼ cupfuls onto a hot, lightly greased griddle. Cook until bubbles appear all over surface. Turn and cook until golden brown.

Sausage and Apple Pancake Bake

Makes 10 to 12 servings

2 eggs
⅔ cup packed brown sugar
1 cup vegetable oil
1 cup buttermilk
2 cups flour
2 cups quick-cooking oats
2 teaspoons baking powder
1 teaspoon salt
1 teaspoon baking soda
1 jar (14 ounces) spiced apple rings, drained; reserve syrup
2 packages (8 ounces each) brown-and-serve sausages
1 cup sugar
¼ cup cornstarch

Preheat oven to 400° F. Grease a 12-cup fluted tube pan; set aside. In a large bowl, combine eggs, brown sugar, oil, and buttermilk; blend well. Stir in flour, oats, baking powder, salt, and baking soda just until blended. Pour ½ cup of the batter into prepared pan. Arrange apple rings on top of batter. Top with sausages. Pour remaining batter over sausages and apple rings. Bake 40 to 50 minutes or until a wooden pick inserted in the center comes out clean. Cool in pan 5 minutes. Invert onto a serving plate. In a small saucepan, combine sugar and cornstarch. In a glass measuring cup, place reserved apple ring syrup. Add water to equal 1 cup. Add liquid to sugar mixture. Cook over low heat until thickened and clear, stirring constantly. Serve with pancake.

Blueberry Sour Cream Pancakes

Makes 16 pancakes

2 cups buttermilk baking mix
1½ cups milk
1 egg
½ cup dairy sour cream
1 cup blueberries
Butter *or* margarine
Syrup

In a small mixing bowl, combine baking mix, milk, egg, and sour cream. Beat on low speed of an electric mixer until just moistened. Pour batter by ¼ cupfuls onto a hot, lightly greased griddle. Sprinkle each pancake with blueberries. Cook until entire surface is bubbly. Turn and cook until golden. Serve with butter and your favorite syrup.

Jams, Jellies, and Marmalades

Plum Conserve

Makes about 2 quarts

- **5 pounds plums, quartered and pitted**
- **1 cup water**
- **1 bag (5 pounds) sugar**
- **¾ pound raisins**
- **2 large oranges**

In a large saucepan or Dutch oven, cook plums in water 10 minutes. Add sugar and raisins; bring to boiling; reduce heat. Boil gently 25 minutes. Grate orange peel; set aside. Squeeze orange juice; add to plums. Simmer 10 minutes. Remove from heat. Stir in orange peel. Ladle into clean hot jars to within ½ inch of the top. Seal with two-piece vacuum seal lids according to manufacturer's directions. Process in boiling water-bath canner for 5 minutes.

Ripe Apricot Jam

Makes about 2½ quarts

- **1¾ pounds apricots, pitted (do not peel)**
- **7 cups sugar**
- **½ bottle liquid pectin**
- **Juice of 1 lemon**

Cut apricots into small pieces; crush or grind in a food mill. Stir in lemon juice. Combine apricots and sugar in a large saucepan or Dutch oven. Bring to boiling, stirring constantly; boil 1 minute. Remove from heat. Stir in liquid pectin; skim top with a spoon. Ladle into clean hot jars to within ½ inch of the top. Seal with two-piece vacuum seal lids according to manufacturer's directions. Process in boiling water-bath canner for 5 minutes.

Scotch Marmalade

Makes 2 quarts

- **4 oranges**
- **2 lemons**
- **2 grapefruit**
- **2½ quarts water**
- **7 cups sugar**

In a large kettle, combine whole fruit and water. Bring to boiling; boil ½ hour. Remove from pan; cool completely. Cut fruit in half; remove pulp. Coarsely chop pulp and fruit peel in a food grinder. Measure chopped fruit and peel. Add enough water to measure 3 quarts. Return to pan. Bring to boiling; boil ¾ hour, stirring frequently. Add sugar. Bring to boiling; boil 15 minutes, stirring often. Ladle into clean hot jars to within ½ inch of the top. Seal with two-piece vacuum seal lids according to manufacturer's directions. Process in boiling water-bath canner for 5 minutes.

One-Two-Three-Four Conserve

Makes about 2 pints

- **1 orange**
- **2 peaches, peeled and chopped**
- **3 cups sugar**
- **4 apples, peeled and chopped**

Cut orange into very small pieces. Grate half of the orange peel. In a medium saucepan, combine orange pieces and peel, peaches, sugar, and apples. Bring to boiling; reduce heat. Cook until thick and fruit is glossy, stirring frequently. Ladle into clean hot jars to within ½ inch of the top. Seal with two-piece vacuum seal lids according to manufacturer's directions. Process in boiling water-bath canner for 5 minutes.

Frozen Strawberry Jam

Makes 3 pints

- **2 quarts strawberries, crushed**
- **4 cups sugar**
- **1 box (1¾ ounces) fruit pectin**
- **¾ cup water**

In a large saucepan or Dutch oven, combine strawberries and sugar; set aside. In a small saucepan, combine pectin and water. Bring to boiling; boil 1 minute, stirring constantly. Stir into strawberry mixture; cook and stir 3 minutes. Ladle into clean hot jars to within ½ inch of the top. Seal with two-piece vacuum seal lids according to manufacturer's directions. Let stand at room temperature 24 hours. Store in freezer.

Kumquat Marmalade

Makes 1 quart

    3 quarts water
    2 cups thinly sliced kumquats
    1½ cups sliced orange peel
    1½ cups chopped orange pulp
    9 cups sugar
    ⅓ cup lemon juice

In a large saucepan or Dutch oven, combine water and fruit. Cover and let stand in a cool place overnight. Bring to boiling; reduce heat. Simmer until orange peel is tender, stirring often. Remove from heat. Measure fruit. For each cup of fruit, add 1 cup sugar; stir until sugar dissolves. Stir in lemon juice. Cook rapidly about 45 minutes or until thickened, stirring occasionally. Ladle into clean hot jars to within ½ inch of the top. Seal with two-piece vacuum seal lids according to manufacturer's directions. Process in boiling water-bath canner for 5 minutes.

Peach Conserve

Makes 1 quart

    1 orange, chopped (do not peel)
    7 cups chopped, peeled, firm-ripe peaches
    5 cups sugar
    ½ teaspoon ground ginger
    ½ cup blanched slivered almonds

In a large saucepan or Dutch oven, combine orange and peaches. Bring to boiling; reduce heat. Simmer 20 minutes, stirring occasionally. Stir in sugar and ginger. Bring to boiling, stirring occasionally, until sugar dissolves. Cook rapidly about 15 minutes or until thickened. As mixture thickens, stir occasionally to prevent sticking. Add nuts the last 5 minutes of cooking time. Ladle into clean hot jars to within ½ inch of the top. Seal with two-piece vacuum seal lids according to manufacturer's directions. Process in boiling water-bath canner for 5 minutes.

Rhubarb Marmalade

Makes 1 quart

    5 cups cut-up rhubarb
    1 cup water
    2 lemons
    ½ cup raisins
    5 cups sugar
    1 cup chopped nuts

In a large saucepan or Dutch oven, combine rhubarb and water. Bring to boiling; boil gently until tender. Squeeze juice from lemons. Grate lemon peel. Add sugar, lemon juice, lemon peel, and raisins to rhubarb; cook until thickened, about 45 minutes. Add nuts during the last 10 minutes of cooking time. Spoon into jars. Ladle into clean hot jars to within ½ inch of the top. Seal with two-piece vacuum seal lids according to manufacturer's directions. Let stand at room temperature 24 hours. Store in refrigerator.

Fresh Apple Butter

Makes 2½ quarts

    6 pounds tart apples
    3 cups water
    Sugar
    1 teaspoon ground cinnamon
    ½ teaspoon ground cloves

Cut apples into quarters. Do not core or peel. Place in a large saucepan or Dutch oven. Add water; cover and cook 30 to 45 minutes or until tender. Press cooked apples through a sieve or food mill. Measure apple pulp. For each cup of pulp, add ½ cup sugar. Stir in cinnamon and cloves. Cook over medium heat until sugar dissolves, stirring often. Simmer, uncovered, over low heat, 1½ to 2 hours stirring occasionally, until apple mixture is thick and smooth when a little is spooned onto a cold plate. Ladle into clean hot jars to within ½ inch of the top. Seal with two-piece vacuum seal lids according to manufacturer's directions. Process in boiling water-bath canner for 5 minutes.

Fruit Medley Preserves

Makes 1½ quarts

    2 cups firmly packed peeled and sliced fresh peaches
    2 cups firmly packed quartered fresh strawberries
    3¾ cups sugar
    1 tablespoon butter
    1 can (13¾ ounces) crushed pineapple, well drained

In a large saucepan or Dutch oven, combine fruit and sugar. Bring to boiling, stirring constantly but gently. Add butter; boil 10 minutes, stirring occasionally. Remove from heat. Stir in pineapple. Pour into a flat pan. Let stand at room temperature overnight. Ladle into clean hot jars to within ½ inch of the top. Seal with two-piece vacuum seal lids according to manufacturer's directions. Process in boiling water-bath canner for 5 minutes.

Pickles and Relishes

Crab Apple Pickles

Makes 1½ quarts

 1½ tablespoons whole cloves
 1½ tablespoons whole allspice
 6 cups sugar
 3 cups vinegar
 3 cups water
 2 cinnamon sticks
 2½ pounds crab apples with stems

Tie spices in a cheesecloth bag. In a large sauce-pan or Dutch oven, combine spice bag, sugar, vinegar, water, and cinnamon sticks. Bring to boiling; boil 5 minutes. Add apples, a layer at a time. Cook gently until apples are almost tender. Carefully remove apples. Repeat until all are cooked. Place apples in a large bowl. Pour boiling syrup over apples. Cover and let stand 12 to 18 hours in a cool place. Carefully pack apples into hot, clean pint jars leaving ¼-inch head space. Discard spice bag. Heat syrup to boiling. Pour over apples, leaving ¼-inch head space. Seal with two-piece vacuum seal lids according to manufacturer's directions. Process in boiling water-bath canner for 15 minutes.

Note: To prevent apples from bursting, pierce with a needle before cooking.

Summer Zucchini Relish

Makes 4 to 6 servings

 4 to 5 medium zucchini
 ½ cup sugar
 ¼ cup honey
 ½ teaspoon salt
 ⅔ cup vinegar
 2 tablespoons vegetable oil
 1 tablespoon minced onion
 ⅓ cup minced green pepper
 ⅓ cup minced celery

Thinly slice zucchini; place in a large bowl. In a separate bowl, combine sugar, honey, salt, vinegar, and oil; blend well. Add onion, green pepper, and celery to zucchini; toss lightly to mix. Pour vinegar mixture over zucchini mixture. Cover and refrigerate at least 4 hours before serving.

Celery and Peppers

Makes 4 to 6 servings

 2 cups diced celery
 ½ cup diced green pepper
 1½ cups water, divided
 1 egg, lightly beaten
 2 tablespoons honey
 2 tablespoons vinegar
 2 tablespoons flour
 ½ teaspoon salt
 ¼ cup dairy sour cream

In a saucepan, combine celery, green pepper, and ½ cup water. Bring to boiling; reduce heat. Simmer until vegetables are tender and water is almost evaporated; set aside. In a separate saucepan, combine egg, honey, vinegar, remaining 1 cup water, flour, and salt. Bring to boiling, stirring constantly; reduce heat. Cook until thickened, stirring constantly. Remove from heat; let stand 10 minutes to cool slightly. Stir in sour cream. Place celery mixture in a serving bowl. Pour sour cream mixture over celery; blend well. Serve immediately.

Pickled Corn

Makes 8 to 10 servings

 1 cup sugar
 ½ cup honey
 2 cups vinegar
 1½ cups water
 1 teaspoon salt
 1 teaspoon celery seed
 ½ teaspoon mustard seed
 1 medium onion, thinly sliced
 4 ears fresh sweet corn, husked and cut in
   1-inch pieces

In a large saucepan, combine sugar, honey, vinegar, water, salt, celery seed, mustard seed, and onion. Bring to boiling; boil 2 minutes. Add corn pieces. Cover and simmer 5 minutes or until corn is tender. Remove from heat. Cool to room temperature. Refrigerate until well chilled.

Pickles and Relishes

Last Harvest Pickles

Makes about 6 pints

      1 cup sliced cucumbers
      1 cup chopped green peppers
      1 cup shredded cabbage
      1 cup sliced onions
      1 cup chopped cored green tomatoes
      ½ cup salt
      2 quarts cold water
      1 cup chopped carrots
      1 cup green beans, cut in 1-inch pieces
      1 cup chopped celery
      2 tablespoons mustard seed
      1 tablespoon celery seed
      2 cups cider vinegar
      2 cups sugar
      2 tablespoons turmeric

In a large bowl, combine cucumbers, green peppers, cabbage, onions, and tomatoes. Prepare a salt brine of ½ cup salt and cold water. Pour over vegetables. Let stand overnight; drain well. In a large saucepan, cook carrots and green beans in 1 inch water until tender; drain well. In a large saucepan or Dutch oven, combine cucumber mixture, carrots, and green beans. Add remaining ingredients. Bring to boiling; boil 10 minutes. Pack into clean hot jars to within ½ inch of the top. Seal with two-piece vacuum seal lids according to manufacturer's directions. Process in boiling water-bath canner for 10 minutes.

Bread-and-Butter Pickles

Makes 7 pints

      25 medium cucumbers, sliced
      12 onions, sliced
      ½ cup pickling salt
      2 cups sugar
      2 teaspoons turmeric
      1 quart vinegar
      2 teaspoons mustard seed
      2 teaspoons celery seed

Soak cucumbers and onions in salted ice water 3 hours. In a large saucepan or Dutch oven, combine remaining ingredients. Heat to boiling. Drain cucumbers and onions. Add to boiling vinegar mixture. Cook 2 minutes without boiling. Pack into clean hot jars to within ½ inch of the top. Seal with two-piece vacuum seal lids according to manufacturer's directions. Process in boiling water-bath canner for 10 minutes.

Green Tomato Relish

Makes about 7 pints

      4 quarts chopped, cored green tomatoes
      2 quarts chopped cabbage
      2 cups chopped sweet red peppers
      1 cup chopped onions
      ½ cup salt
      4½ cups vinegar
      1½ cups packed brown sugar
      2 tablespoons mustard seed
      1 tablespoon celery seed
      1 tablespoon prepared horseradish

In a large bowl, combine vegetables and salt; mix well. Let stand 3 to 4 hours. Drain well; squeeze out excess liquid. In a large saucepan or Dutch oven, combine vinegar, brown sugar, spices, and horseradish. Bring to boiling; reduce heat. Simmer 15 minutes. Add vegetables; bring to boiling. Pack into clean hot jars to within ½ inch of the top. Seal with two-piece vacuum seal lids according to manufacturer's directions. Process in boiling water-bath canner for 10 minutes.

Tart Cherry Relish

Makes 2½ cups

      1 can (20 ounces) tart red cherries, pitted
      ½ cup raisins
      ½ cup honey
      ¼ cup cider vinegar
      ¼ cup packed brown sugar
      ½ teaspoon ground cinnamon
      ⅛ teaspoon ground cloves
      ½ cup chopped pecans
      1 tablespoon cornstarch
      1 tablespoon cold water

In a 2-quart saucepan, combine cherries, raisins, honey, vinegar, brown sugar, cinnamon, and cloves. Cook slowly, uncovered, 30 minutes, stirring occasionally. Stir in pecans. Dissolve cornstarch in water. Gradually stir cornstarch mixture into cherry mixture. Cook until mixture thickens and bubbles, stirring constantly. Chill well before serving.

Easy Custard Pie

Makes 6 to 8 servings

4 eggs, lightly beaten
½ cup sugar
¼ teaspoon salt
1 teaspoon vanilla
2½ cups milk, scalded
1 unbaked 9-inch piecrust (recipe on this page)
Dash nutmeg

In a mixing bowl, combine eggs, sugar, salt, and vanilla; blend well. Slowly stir in hot milk. Pour into piecrust. Sprinkle with nutmeg. Bake at 475° F. 5 minutes. Reduce heat to 425° F. and bake 10 minutes or until a knife inserted near the center comes out clean. Cool on a wire rack.

Note: To avoid spilling after filling piecrust, place piecrust on oven rack before filling with custard.

Chocolate Cream Pie

Makes 6 to 8 servings

1 envelope unflavored gelatin
¼ cup cold water
1 cup milk, scalded
6 tablespoons unsweetened cocoa
½ cup sugar
½ teaspoon salt
1 teaspoon vanilla
1 cup whipping cream, whipped
1 baked 9-inch piecrust (recipe on this page)
Sweetened whipped cream, optional

In a small bowl, soften gelatin in cold water. In a saucepan, scald milk. Add cocoa, sugar, and salt; blend well. Slowly stir into gelatin mixture until gelatin dissolves. Let stand until mixture begins to thicken. Stir in vanilla. Fold in whipped cream until no streaks of white remain. Pour into baked piecrust. Chill until set. Garnish with sweetened whipped cream before serving, if desired.

Sweet Potato Pudding

Makes 4 servings

3 eggs
1½ cups milk
1½ cups sugar
⅛ teaspoon salt
4 cups grated raw sweet potatoes
½ cup butter *or* margarine, melted
Grated peel of 1 orange
2 teaspoons vanilla

In a mixing bowl, combine eggs, milk, sugar, and salt; blend well. Add potatoes, butter, orange peel, and vanilla; blend well. Turn into a buttered 2-quart baking dish. Bake, uncovered, 45 minutes or until set.

Pink Ribbon Apple Pie

Makes 1 pie

Piecrust (recipe follows)
8 to 9 tart apples, peeled and cored
¼ cup lemon juice
1½ to 2 cups sugar
3 tablespoons flour
1 teaspoon salt
1 teaspoon ground cinnamon
½ teaspoon ground nutmeg
Butter

Slice apples; place in a bowl of ice water with lemon juice. Prepare piecrust. Divide dough. Roll out one half on a floured pastry cloth 1 inch larger than a 9-inch pie plate. Fit dough into pie plate. Drain apples on paper towels. Place a layer of apples in prepared pie plate. In a small bowl, combine sugar, flour, salt, cinnamon, and nutmeg; blend well. Sprinkle some of the sugar mixture over apple layer; dot with butter. Repeat layers until all apples are used, ending with sugar mixture and butter. Roll out remaining dough. Place on top of apples. Press top and bottom crusts together; trim and flute edge. Cut slits in the top to vent steam. Bake on middle rack in oven at 400° F. 10 minutes. Reduce heat to 350° F. and bake 40 minutes or until bubbly and golden.

Note: For easy clean-up, place a piece of aluminum foil on the bottom shelf of the oven to catch overflow.

Piecrust

1 cup vegetable shortening
3 cups sifted flour
1½ teaspoons salt
½ cup ice water

In a mixing bowl, cut shortening into flour and salt using a pastry blender or two knives until consistency of small peas. Blend in water, 1 tablespoon at a time, tossing with a fork. Gather dough into a ball.

Fresh Cherry Pie

Makes 6 to 8 servings

　1 recipe Piecrust (page 57)
1⅓ to 1½ cups sugar
　⅓ cup flour
　⅛ teaspoon salt
　4 cups pitted tart cherries
　3 drops almond extract, optional
　2 tablespoons butter *or* margarine

Prepare piecrust. Divide dough in half. Roll out half on a lightly floured surface to 1 inch larger than an inverted 9-inch pie plate. Fit crust into pie plate. Trim edge; set aside. In a small bowl, combine sugar, flour and salt; set aside. In a separate bowl, combine cherries and almond extract. Sprinkle with flour mixture; toss lightly to mix. Turn cherry mixture into prepared crust. Roll out remaining dough. Cut into ½-inch strips. Weave strips into a lattice top. Trim, seal, and flute edge. Bake at 425° F. about 40 minutes or until bubbly.

Apricot Cake Treat

Makes 6 servings

　¾ pound dried apricots
　½ cup sugar
　2 tablespoons orange juice
　½ cup slivered almonds
　1 cup whipping cream, whipped
　1 package lady fingers, split
　　Sweetened whipped cream, optional

In a heavy saucepan, combine apricots and water to cover. Bring to boiling; reduce heat. Simmer 25 minutes, stirring often. Add sugar; cook 5 minutes, stirring constantly. In an electric blender or food processor, puree apricots. Add more sugar to taste. Allow to cool. Stir in orange juice, almonds, and whipped cream. Line a large bowl with split ladyfingers. Spoon apricot mixture into bowl. Chill 1 hour. Serve with sweetened whipped cream, if desired.

Potato Cake

Makes 12 servings

　1 cup butter *or* margarine, softened
　2 cups sugar
　4 eggs, separated
　1 cup unseasoned mashed potatoes
　1 cup chopped nuts
　1 teaspoon ground cinnamon
　1 teaspoon ground cloves
　1 teaspoon ground nutmeg
2½ cups flour
　2 teaspoons baking powder
　½ cup milk

Grease and flour a 13 x 9-inch baking pan; set aside. Preheat oven to 350° F. In a large mixing bowl, cream butter and sugar with an electric mixer until light and fluffy. Add egg yolks, potatoes, nuts, and spices; blend well. In a separate bowl, combine flour and baking powder. Alternately add flour mixture and milk to creamed mixture; blend well. In a small bowl, beat egg whites with electric mixer until stiff peaks form. Gently fold egg whites into batter. Pour batter into prepared pan. Bake 45 minutes or until a toothpick inserted in the center comes out clean.

Pumpkin Bars

Makes 36 bars

　4 eggs
　1 cup vegetable oil
　2 cups sugar
　1 can (15 ounces) pumpkin
　2 cups flour
　2 teaspoons baking powder
　1 teaspoon baking soda
　½ teaspoon salt
　2 teaspoons ground cinnamon
　½ teaspoon ground ginger
　½ teaspoon ground cloves
　½ teaspoon ground nutmeg
　½ cup chopped nuts
　　Cream Cheese Frosting (recipe on page 63)

Grease and flour an 18 x 12-inch baking pan; set aside. Preheat oven to 350° F. In a large mixing bowl, combine eggs, oil, sugar, and pumpkin; blend well. In a separate bowl, sift together flour, baking powder, baking soda, salt, and spices. Gradually beat flour mixture into pumpkin mixture. Stir in nuts. Pour batter into prepared pan. Bake 25 to 30 minutes or until center springs back when touched lightly. Cool on a wire rack before frosting with Cream Cheese Frosting.

Desserts

Date Chocolate Chip Bars

Makes 12 servings

    1 package (8 ounces) pitted dates, chopped
    ½ cup sugar
    1 cup water
    ⅔ cup butter or margarine
    1 cup packed brown sugar
    1½ cups quick-cooking oats
    1 teaspoon baking soda
    1 tablespoon hot water
    1½ cups flour
    ½ cup chopped nuts
    ½ cup semisweet chocolate chips
      Sweetened whipped cream, optional

In a medium saucepan, combine dates, sugar, and water. Cook over medium heat until thick, stirring constantly. In a mixing bowl, combine butter and brown sugar. Cream with an electric mixer until light and fluffy. Add oats, baking soda, and hot water; blend well. Gradually add flour; blend well. Reserve 1 cup crumb mixture for topping. Press remaining crumb mixture into an ungreased 13 x 9-inch baking pan. Spread date mixture evenly over top. Sprinkle with nuts, chocolate chips, and reserved crumb mixture; pat lightly. Bake at 350° F. 20 to 25 minutes or until golden. Serve warm or cool topped with whipped cream, if desired.

Grandma's Peanut Butter Cookies

Makes about 5 dozen

    1 cup butter or margarine
    1 cup peanut butter
    1 cup granulated sugar
    1 cup packed brown sugar
    2 eggs, lightly beaten
    1 teaspoon vanilla
    2 cups flour
    1 teaspoon salt
    1 teaspoon baking soda

In a mixing bowl, cream butter and peanut butter until well blended. Add sugars; cream until light and fluffy. Beat in eggs and vanilla. In a separate bowl, sift together flour, salt, and baking soda. Gradually add to creamed mixture; blend well. Roll dough into 1-inch balls. Place balls, 2 inches apart, on a large baking sheet. Press with tines of a fork to flatten. Bake at 350° F. about 10 minutes or until golden. Cool on a wire rack.

Sugar Cookies

Makes 6 dozen

    1 cup granulated sugar
    1 cup powdered sugar
    1 cup butter or margarine
    1 cup vegetable oil
    2 eggs
    1 teaspoon baking soda
    1 teaspoon cream of tartar
    ½ teaspoon salt
    1 teaspoon vanilla
    4½ cups flour
      Granulated sugar

In a large mixing bowl, combine sugars, butter, oil, and eggs; beat until well blended. Beat in baking soda, cream of tartar, salt, and vanilla. Gradually add flour; beat until well blended. Cover and chill well. Roll dough into 1-inch balls. Roll balls in granulated sugar. Place balls 2 inches apart on a baking sheet. Flatten with the bottom of a glass. Bake at 375° F. 10 to 12 minutes. Cool on a wire rack.

Best Fudge Nut Brownies

Makes 9 brownies

    4 squares (1 ounce each) unsweetened baking
      chocolate
    1 cup butter or margarine, softened
    2 cups sugar
    3 eggs, lightly beaten
    2 teaspoons vanilla
    ½ teaspoon salt
    1 cup chopped nuts
    1 cup sifted flour

Preheat oven to 350° F. In a small saucepan, melt chocolate and butter over low heat, stirring constantly. Add sugar and eggs; blend well. Stir in vanilla, salt, and nuts. Gradually add flour; blend well. Pour into a greased and floured 9-inch square baking pan. Bake 40 to 45 minutes or until brownie begins to pull away from edge of pan. Cool in pan on a wire rack. Cut into squares.

Rhubarb Custard Dessert

Makes 16 servings

　　Crust (recipe follows)
　6 eggs, separated
2¾ cups sugar, divided
　1 cup half-and-half *or* milk*
　¼ cup flour
　6 cups cut-up rhubarb
　½ cup chopped nuts, optional
　½ cup shredded coconut, optional

Prepare crust; pat into an 18 x 12-inch baking pan. Bake at 350° F. 10 minutes. Remove from oven; let stand until cool. In a large mixing bowl, combine egg yolks, 2 cups sugar, half-and-half, and flour; blend well. Stir in rhubarb. Pour custard mixture evenly over cooled crust. Bake at 350° F. 40 minutes or until set. In a small mixing bowl, beat egg whites with an electric mixer until foamy. Gradually add remaining ¾ cup sugar, beating until stiff peaks form. Spread meringue on top of rhubarb custard, being certain to seal edges. Sprinkle with nuts and coconut, if desired. Bake 10 to 12 minutes or until lightly browned.

*If using milk, add 1 whole egg to custard.

Crust

　1 cup vegetable shortening
　2 cups flour
　2 tablespoons sugar

In a mixing bowl, cut shortening into flour and sugar using a pastry blender or two knives until consistency of coarse crumbs.

Note: Recipe can be cut in half and baked in a 9-inch baking pan.

Red Buttermilk Cake

Makes 12 servings

　½ cup butter *or* margarine
1½ cups sugar
　2 eggs
　2 teaspoons unsweetened cocoa
　2 ounces red food coloring
2½ cups cake flour
　1 teaspoon salt
　1 cup buttermilk
　1 teaspoon vanilla
　1 teaspoon baking soda
　1 teaspoon vinegar
　　Buttercream Icing (recipe follows)

Grease and flour three 9-inch round baking pans; set aside. Preheat oven to 350° F. In a mixing bowl, cream butter, sugar, and eggs with an elec-

tric mixer until light and fluffy. In a small bowl, combine cocoa and food coloring; blend to make a paste. Add to creamed mixture; blend well. Sift flour and salt together. Alternately add flour mixture and buttermilk to creamed mixture; blend well after each addition. Blend in vanilla. Beat on medium speed 8 to 10 minutes until smooth. In a small bowl, combine baking soda and vinegar. Blend into batter at low speed. Pour into prepared pans. Bake 30 minutes or until a wooden pick inserted in the center comes out clean. Cool in pans 10 minutes. Invert onto a wire rack to cool completely. Fill layers with Buttercream Icing. Spread sides and top with icing.

Buttercream Icing

　5 tablespoons flour
1½ cups sugar, divided
　1 cup milk
　1 cup butter *or* margarine
　1 teaspoon vanilla

In a small saucepan, combine flour, ½ cup sugar and milk; blend until smooth. Cook over medium heat until thickened, stirring constantly. Let stand until cool. In a small mixing bowl, cream remaining sugar, butter, and vanilla until light and fluffy, about 15 minutes. Gradually beat in cooled milk mixture. Beat until smooth and fluffy.

Light Peanut Brittle

Makes about 1 pound

　1 cup light corn syrup
　½ cup water
　2 cups sugar
　　Dash salt
　1 cup butter
　2 cups unsalted peanuts
　2 teaspoons vanilla
　1 teaspoon baking soda

Butter 2 large baking sheets; set aside. In a heavy saucepan, combine corn syrup, water, sugar, and salt. Cook over low heat until sugar dissolves, stirring frequently. Bring to boiling; add butter. Cook, without stirring, until 235° F. on a candy thermometer, then stir occasionally. Add nuts when temperature reaches 280° F. Cook, stirring constantly, until 305° F. Remove from heat. Quickly stir in vanilla and baking soda. Pour onto prepared baking sheets. Lift and pull from edges with fork to stretch. As soon as candy sets, loosen from pan. Break into pieces.

Carrot Cake

Makes 12 servings

2 cups flour
2 teaspoons baking soda
2 teaspoons ground cinnamon
1½ teaspoons salt
2 cups sugar
1½ cups vegetable oil
4 eggs
1 tablespoon vanilla
3 cups grated carrots
1 cup chopped pitted dates
1 cup flaked coconut
1 cup raisins, optional
1 cup chopped nuts, optional
Cream Cheese Frosting (recipe follows)

In a large bowl, sift together flour, baking soda, cinnamon, and salt; set aside. In a large mixing bowl, combine sugar and oil; blend well. Beat in eggs, one at a time, until well blended. Stir in vanilla. Gradually add dry ingredients; beat until well blended. Stir in carrots, dates, coconut, raisins, and nuts, if desired. Pour batter into a greased 13 x 9-inch baking pan. Bake at 350° F. 30 to 40 minutes or until center springs back when lightly touched. Cool on a wire rack. Frost with Cream Cheese Frosting.

Cream Cheese Frosting

2 packages (3 ounces each) cream cheese, softened
6 tablespoons butter *or* margarine, softened
1 tablespoon milk
1 teaspoon vanilla
4 cups sifted powdered sugar

In a mixing bowl, combine cream cheese and butter; cream with electric mixer until light and fluffy. Beat in milk and vanilla. Gradually beat in powdered sugar until of spreading consistency.

Jelly Roll

Makes 8 servings

3 eggs
1 cup sugar
1 cup sifted cake flour
1 teaspoon baking powder
¼ teaspoon salt
⅓ cup hot water
1 teaspoon vanilla
Powdered sugar
1 jar (10 ounces) strawberry *or* raspberry jelly

Preheat oven to 375° F. In a mixing bowl, beat eggs with an electric mixer until thick and light-colored. Gradually beat in sugar. In a separate bowl, sift together flour, baking powder, and salt. With mixer on low speed, blend in dry ingredients, water, and vanilla until just mixed. Grease and flour a 15 x 10-inch jelly-roll pan. Pour batter into prepared pan. Bake 15 to 20 minutes or until cake begins to shrink slightly from edge of pan. Turn cake out onto a clean towel lightly dusted with powdered sugar; trim edges. Spread jelly over cake; roll up, from long side. Wrap in towel. Cool on a wire rack. Sprinkle lightly with powdered sugar. Slice and serve.

Poppy Seed Torte

Makes 15 servings

¾ cup poppy seed
¾ cup warm milk
1½ cups sugar
¾ cup butter *or* margarine, softened
2 cups flour
2 teaspoons baking powder
4 egg whites
Custard Filling (recipe follows)
Powdered sugar

In a small bowl, combine poppy seed and warm milk; let stand overnight. In a large mixing bowl, cream sugar and butter until light and fluffy. In a separate bowl sift together flour and baking powder. Alternately add dry ingredients and poppy seed mixture; blend well. In a small mixing bowl, beat egg whites until stiff peaks form. Gently fold egg whites into batter. Preheat oven to 350° F. Grease and flour two 9-inch baking pans. Pour batter into prepared pans. Bake 30 to 35 minutes or until golden. Cool slightly in pans. Turn out of pans onto a wire rack. Split each layer in half. Fill layers with Custard Filling. Lightly sift powdered sugar on top.

Custard Filling

2 cups milk
1 cup sugar
2 tablespoons cornstarch
4 egg yolks

In a saucepan, combine milk, sugar, and cornstarch; stir to dissolve cornstarch. Cook over low heat until thickened, stirring constantly. Remove from heat. In a small bowl, beat egg yolks with an electric mixer until light-colored. Stir a little of the hot mixture into the egg yolks to warm. Gradually return egg yolks to hot mixture. Let stand until cool.

Jelly Roll

Index